Sinister Wisdom 127
Winter 2023

Publisher: Sinister Wisdom, Inc.
Editor & Publisher: Julie R. Enszer
Associate Editor: Sierra Earle
Guest Editor: Susannah Magers
Assistant Editor: Ivy Clarke
Graphic Designer: Nieves Guerra
Copy Editor: Ivy Clarke
Board of Directors: Roberta Arnold, Cheryl Clarke, Julie R. Enszer, Sara Gregory, Yeva Johnson, Shromona Mandal, Joan Nestle, Rose Norman, Mecca Jamilah Sullivan, Yasmin Tambiah, and Red Washburn

Front cover and back cover Art: Lukaza Branfman-Verissimo. *Our People Should be Prioritized*, 2019.

Media: Acrylic, gouache, flash, chalkboard paint, and colored pencil on panel, 60" x 60".

Artist biography: Lukaza Branfman-Verissimo (they/them/Lukaza) is an artist, activist, educator, storyteller & curator who lives/works between Lisjan Ohlone Land [Oakland, CA] and Powhatan Land [Richmond, VA]. They got their MFA from Virginia Commonwealth University and BFA from California College of the Arts. Branfman-Verissimo's work has been included in exhibitions and performances at Konsthall C [Stockholm, Sweden], SEPTEMBER Gallery [Kinderhook, NY], EFA Project Space [New York City, NY], Leslie Lohman Museum [New York City, NY], Yerba Buena Center for the Arts [San Francisco, CA] and Berkeley Art Museum and Pacific Film Archive [Berkeley, CA], amongst others. Their artist books and prints have been published by Endless Editions, Childish Books, Play Press, Press Press, Sming Sming and Night Diver Press. They are a current member of Moments Co-op and Community Space [Oakland, CA] and Book/Print of Color Collective. Image copyright 2023.

SINISTER WISDOM, founded 1976
Former editors and publishers:
Harriet Ellenberger (aka Desmoines) and Catherine Nicholson (1976–1981)
Michelle Cliff and Adrienne Rich (1981–1983)
Michaele Uccella (1983–1984)
Melanie Kaye/Kantrowitz (1983–1987)
Elana Dykewomon (1987–1994)
Caryatis Cardea (1991–1994)
Akiba Onada-Sikwoia (1995–1997)
Margo Mercedes Rivera-Weiss (1997–2000)
Fran Day (2004–2010)
Julie R. Enszer & Merry Gangemi (2010–2013)
Julie R. Enszer (2013–)

Copyright © 2023 *Sinister Wisdom*, Inc.
All rights revert to individual authors and artists upon publication.
Printed in the U. S. on recycled paper.

Subscribe online: www.SinisterWisdom.org
Join *Sinister Wisdom* on Facebook: www.Facebook.com/SinisterWisdom
Follow *Sinister Wisdom* on Instagram: www.Instagram.com/sinister_wisdom
Follow *Sinister Wisdom* on Twitter: www.twitter.com/Sinister_Wisdom
Sinister Wisdom is a US non-profit organization; donations to support the work and distribution of *Sinister Wisdom* are welcome and appreciated.
Consider including *Sinister Wisdom* in your will.

Sinister Wisdom, 2333 McIntosh Road, Dover, FL 33527-5980 USA

TABLE OF CONTENTS

Notes for a Magazine 7

On Transfer

Notes for a Special Issue 11

Shawn(ta) Smith-Cruz
   On Celebrating Trust and Transfer
      of the Salsa Soul Sisters Archive 15

Nomi F. Beesen
   Things I Lost at Q Bar 29
   Things I Looked for at Metropolitan Bar 30

Camila Coddou
   On Nonlinear Journeys and Advocating
      for Yourself and Others 31

Welly Fletcher
   On Monuments and Inventing Other Building Blocks 49

Karen Poppy
   Diving at the Lip of the Water 64

Maddy Court
   On Niche Lesbian Content, Internet Communities,
      and Queer Advice 70

Anna Olver
   Cluster 82

Lenn Keller
   On Black butch visibility 83

Elizabeth Train-Brown
   The Dead Letter Office 90
   Glimpse 93
   Brisk 'O 94

Kara Q. Smith
　On Maintaining a Sustainable Creative Practice
　　　and Carrying Loose Ends 95
Mev Miller
　Cherishing/Guarding Lesbiana:
　　A Movement of Words on the Page 108
Julie R. Enszer
　On Moving *Sinister Wisdom* Across the Country 114
Sarah Werthmann
　Anteriority Rose Like Bile 121
Lynn Harris Ballen
　On building Generational Bridges Through Creative
　　　Collaboration 122
　Installation Images From *Political Birthdays* 141

New Lesbian Writing

Bronwyn Hughes
　The Kittiwake 149
Evelyn C White
　Charm Bracelet 160
Sydney Bernthold
　Elegy for the Best Drag Queen to Come Out
　　　of the Appalachian Mountains 161
Barbara McBane
　Irresistible Anchovies 163
Josie Pierce
　Venus 165
Adela Zamudio,
Translated From The Spanish By Lynette Yetter
　Yesterday Afternoon 167
Tova Vitiello
　Awakening 170

Jess Saldaña
    Microtear 172
Mischa Kuczynski
    Name You 174
    First Kiss 175
    Vestigial 176
Sofía Ivy Ripley
    Them III 177
Shelby Griffin
    Camp/Play 179
Barbara Rosen
    Friendship 183
    It Was Dark 184
    A Precarious Love 185
    Our Hearts Are As One 186
    One Lesbian Life 187
Fable Todd
    sometimes my friends are annoyed
        by how often i say "lesbian" 191

Rose Norman
    Remembrance: Sue Parker "Rainbow" Williams (1934-2022) .. 193

    Book Reviews 199

NOTES FOR A MAGAZINE

In lesbian communities right now, often anxiety is high about change. We look around with concern, even fear, about communal evolutions which seem to shift the ground beneath our feet. We worry about what future holds and wonder if we will recognize the generations of lesbians, or as they often call themselves queer women, who will come after us. I understand the concerns. We continue to live in a heteropatriarchy fueled by virulent capitalism and with growing right-wing extremism. These are not easy times for lesbians, for women, for queer people, especially for those who are Indigenous, African-American, Latinx, Asian-American, or people of color.

Yet, I continue to maintain that fear, anxiety, and worry are not the answers. In spite of the political, economic, and social challenges that we face individually and communally, lesbian and queer women's communities are vibrant, growing, and thriving. We continue to create art, literature, and community. We show up for one another to support, dream, challenge, and imagine new worlds for lesbians and new ways to express and name ourselves, our lovers, our desires, and our lives. This issue of *Sinister Wisdom*, *Sinister Wisdom* 127: *On Transfer* demonstrates the vibrancy of change and transfer for lesbians.

Susannah Magers has assembled a vital collection of interviews and creative work that ponders transfer: what we give to and receive from one another in lesbian communities. Part of the excitement of this issue for me is the ways it considers generational transfer in pieces like Shawn Smith-Cruz's reflections on the Salsa Soul Sisters, Lenn Keller's interview, and Lynn Harris Ballen on building generational bridges through creative collaborations. These folks thinking about transfer across generations inspire me to continue the work of *Sinister Wisdom*. These women remind me that out there in the world right now is the next editor of the journal, thinking, growing, waiting to breathe life into it for new generations. (I'm sticking around a while—don't worry!—but I like knowing that she/they are out there!)

Recently, a summer intern and I in conversation with a variety of guest editors completed a new editorial guide for folks interested in editing an issue of *Sinister Wisdom*. In that guide, we echo what *Sinister Wisdom* publishes from our website, and I added the line that at *Sinister Wisdom*, identity language, the language that we use to define, assert, and conjure ourselves as lesbian communities, is broad, capacious, emergent, ever-evolving, and always under discussion. Reading our now large archive reminds me of the many conversations about identity—and transfer. I am glad the conversation continues.

As always a huge thank you to everyone who showed up to *Sinister Wisdom's* annual fundraiser in the fall. I am grateful to everyone who subscribes, donates, and gives of their time, talent, and treasure to keep *Sinister Wisdom* vibrant.

In sisterhood,
Julie

Julie R Enszer, PhD
January 2023

On Transfer

NOTES FOR A SPECIAL ISSUE

I began to envision this issue in the spring of 2017, at a personal and professional crossroads. This period was both the high and low of my art career. I'd moved to a town in the upper Midwest for a coveted full-time curatorial gig, a goal I'd dedicated over a decade of my life, including four years of college, two years of graduate school, and a mountain of student loan debt to — only to discover shortly thereafter it was wildly dysfunctional, toxic, and had a staff revolving door. I stuck it out as long as I could but eventually landed back in California, the state where I was born and had spent half of my life in.

During this time, I reevaluated everything. I was burnt out, demoralized, and wondering if I should keep going with my pursuit of a creative career. On a global level, we were a year into the T***p presidency, watching in collective horror and fury as the LGTBQ+ page disappeared from the website of the "highest" office in the country and the culture wars were revived once again.

It was also at this time that I discovered *Sinister Wisdom* and felt a renewed sense of purpose. Receiving the news that the journal's archives were recently transferred from the Bay Area of California to Florida — a literal transfer — I began a conversation with Julie on the conceptual framework and potential of transferring. I was fascinated by the fact that the journal would move to wherever the current editor called home. I also started the journal's Instagram account, sharing highlights from past issues, celebrating independent bookstores that carried *Sinister Wisdom*, and spreading the word about the journal and community. Thanks to social media (I'm both an advocate and a detractor), there was an online renaissance of lesbian culture, a rise in accounts that unearthed our herstories and gave them visibility in ways they never had before. I wanted *Sinister Wisdom* to be a part of that.

In her 2005 "Notes for a Magazine" for *Sinister Wisdom 64: Lesbians and Music, Drama, and Art*, former *Sinister Wisdom* editor Fran Day wrote: "The pieces in this issue frame important questions about the political potential of the visual and performing arts to inspire us as individuals and to change the world." Inspired by Day's words, and with an emphasis on interviews and creative practice, *On Transfer* pays specific attention to the idea of intentional transfer as an essential component in artmaking, cultural production, and building community.

While written over four years ago at the time of writing this, the call for submissions remains relevant as ever: As we continue to show up, be visible, push against, and shape our communities — and a world — we want to inhabit, what do we pass on or transfer to each other? How do we connect with, motivate, and inspire — especially in times like these? What are the ways in which we shift and change along the way, and what lessons have we learned — or, in some cases, unlearned?

The writing, art, and interviews in this issue represent specific moments in transfer: some over a year, others a lifetime. Snapshots of collaborations, records of relationships, (re)considerations of impacts. Being in the throes of transformation and coming out on the other side. Personal and professional journeys, triumphs, and failures. The projects, dreams, calls to action, and conversations here represent stages in a process.

At a songwriter round I recently attended — the first public gathering my wife and I tepidly agreed to brave in over two years, which still felt uneasy despite vaccination requirements and masks — four musicians took turns baring their souls, fears, and hopes in new songs and old. One shared a piece about the passage of time in a pandemic and the nagging feeling that you should be doing something with it — something productive and meaningful — only you can't. The feeling of being stuck inside ourselves, our minds, with our doubt and uncertainty since March 2020 (it is now almost that same time in 2022 as I write this). The statement felt like a kind of permission to resist the inertia of productivity culture and resulting guilt that if you were privileged enough to get to stay home, you better have done something. The song was a reminder to be gentle to yourself. That getting up and making it through another day was enough.

I want to acknowledge that creative block, one I've acutely struggled with as I worked to finish this issue. When the pandemic hit and we couldn't know (or comprehend) that weeks of isolation and the world shutting down would stretch into months, and then years — like many, I tried to assuage my anxiety with aspirations of how much I would get done. I would read that book I borrowed from a friend months ago that was collecting dust on my bedside table. I would finally start painting again and spend more time outside instead of at a desk. I would finish the outreach and interviews for this issue and *absolutely* make the most of these circumstances. But I became consumed with the news, with the cleaning and prevention rituals. Buying groceries was an event we geared up for and decompressed from after. We couldn't calm down and our nervous systems were (and in many ways still are) in a constant state of hyperarousal. Had we sanitized enough? Did I forget to shower and wash everything I wore after that last trip to buy toilet paper? Were we, and our friends, and our neighbors, going to be ok?

This project, like our lives, has been through many stages of transfer over the past four years. Thank you to all of the contributors who gave their time, spirit, and energy and shared their creative visions and notions of transfer with me, to Lukaza for gracing the covers with her exquisite artwork, and a huge thank you to Julie Enszer for her patience and guidance as I pushed through blocks of every shape and size to get this issue finished and out in the world.

Let's keep transferring and listening to our stories and learning from and showing up for each other.

In solidarity and with care,
Susannah

Susannah Magers (she/her) has built a life around creativity and community. Though her "day job" is now mostly in marketing, she worked in the art world for over a decade: first as a photographer, and then as an art curator, exhibition manager, and program director. Past roles include Deputy Director and Curator at Rochester Art Center, in MN, and Interpretation Manager for the site-specific public art exhibition @*Large: Ai Weiwei on Alcatraz*. Curatorial projects include the 2016 exhibition *Amanda Curreri: The Calmest of Us Would Be Lunatics*, which was also presented as part of a panel at the Oakland Museum of California, during Open Engagement 2016—POWER; the 2018 group exhibition *Political Birthdays* inspired by a Jeanne Córdova quote about political activism, identity, and self expression at Dream Farm Commons in downtown Oakland, CA; and the 2018 group exhibition *Material Futurity* at the Law Warschaw Gallery at Macalester College, St. Paul, MN.

A former co-director of Oakland project space Royal NoneSuch Gallery, she holds a dual BA in Art and History from the University of California, Santa Cruz, and an MA in Curatorial Practice from the California College of the Arts, San Francisco, CA — please reach out to her if you are considering taking out loans for graduate school.

Susannah started the *Sinister Wisdom* Instagram account and contributed an edited interview between artist Amanda Curreri and frequent editor and contributor (including this issue!) Shawn(ta) Smith-Cruz about the experience of researching and working from queer archives which appeared in *Sinister Wisdom 101: Variations*.

From Northern California, Susannah now calls coastal New England home where she spends her free time dreaming up next home projects with her wife, exploring the Maine wilderness with their rescue dog, devouring queer film and media, combing antique stores for vintage treasures, and reading, writing about, collecting, and experiencing art. She's working to set up an arts residency in a large future hybrid project and living space above her garage to support queer creatives.

ON CELEBRATING TRUST AND TRANSFER OF THE SALSA SOUL SISTERS ARCHIVE
— A *conversation with Shawn(ta) Smith-Cruz*

Shawn(ta) Smith-Cruz is an archivist at the Lesbian Herstory Archives, an Assistant Curator and Associate Dean for Teaching, Learning, and Engagement at New York University Division of Libraries. Shawn has a BS in Queer Women's Studies from the CUNY Baccalaureate Program, an MFA in Creative Writing/Fiction, and an MLS with a focus on Archiving and Records Management from Queens College. She is the 2020 recipient of the WGSS Award for Significant Achievement, sponsored by Duke University Press, administered by the Association of College and Research Libraries (ACRL), a division of the American Libraries Association, for her work archiving and exhibiting the Salsa Soul Sisters, the first lesbian of color organization in the country.

Her writing is featured in journals and anthologies such as *Reference Librarianship & Justice: History, Practice and Praxis* (2018), *Informed Agitation: Library and Information Skills in Social Justice Movements and Beyond* (2014), *Frontiers: A Journal of Women's Studies* (2013), *Out Behind the Desk: Workplace Issues for LGBTQ Librarians* (2011), *Films for the Feminist Classroom* (2010), and others. She is also a Zinester, disseminating her Zine, *Black Lesbians in the 70's and Before: An at Home Tour at the Lesbian Herstory Archives.*

SSC: Over 10 years ago, I was on a panel at the LGBTQ Community Center, formerly known as the Lesbian and Gay Center in Manhattan. It was run through AALUSC (African Ancestral Lesbians United for Societal Change). I find that, in the history of the organization, most of what I know about them is that they're always sort of trying to get it together. Like, that's always the narrative: we're meeting to meet, we're meeting to figure out how we're going to meet, we're meeting to figure out what's happening and to reinvigorate our organization. And that's what they're always doing, which is interesting. So, the AALUSC panel was about what was happening in Black lesbian organizing in New York City. In 2009, I sat on a panel with Olive Demetrius and Hanifah Walidah, who did a documentary called *U People* (2008). They were a power couple at the time but have since broken up. Another young woman sat on the panel whose name I can't remember; she was working on a social media documentary or YouTube series. Cassandra Grant was on the panel, and she was representing the Salsa Soul Sisters, the organization that AALUSC came out of. In fact, AALUSC's banner included, in parentheses, "formerly Salsa Soul." Cassandra introduced Salsa Soul Sisters to the community, and I still remember she was holding these papers and clutching them, and they were a bit disheveled. It was almost like she was, like, grabbing things to go. And she was like, "This is our archive. And I need some sister to come and collect our archive."

SM: She was holding the archive in her hands?

SCC: Yep. And I was sort of like, yeah, I'll do it. She said she had more at home, but she was the person who was bestowed the papers, and she doesn't trust it to go just anywhere. She talked to the Schomburg Center for Research in Black Culture at the New York Public Library, but she doesn't know, and she wants someone to take an interest, to gather and collect. The Schomburg Center would have been a likely spot for the Salsa Soul Sisters' collection. I'm not sure why they didn't send it there. Maybe there was an interest. Maybe they couldn't get it together. I'm not sure, but I sort of took it to heart. And then I thought, well, I'm a coordinator at the Lesbian Herstory Archives, maybe this is something I'll look into later.

The following year, in 2010, I was also working at the Center for LGBTQ Studies at the time as a Memberships and Fellowships Coordinator on a conference called *In Amerika They Called Us*

Dykes: Lesbian Lives in the 70s. That's its own story, but the goal was to have lesbians from the seventies return and recall this time. It was supposed to unfold over a full year, so there'd be a spring series and a fall festival. It was meant to be coordinated by lesbians from the seventies and as one of two staff people that was helping put it together, I coordinated a listserv and dealt with logistics. But when I was in one of the planning meetings, there was a conversation around how we would include representation of Black lesbians. Someone had alluded that there were no Black lesbians in the seventies.

SM: What?!

SCC: I know, right?! And others *agreed* with that. In *Sinister Wisdom* 107: *Black Lesbians / We are the Revolution!* I wrote about the zine I made that came from that conversation. So, for the 2010 CLAGS conference, there was an event every month in the spring, followed by a fall festival. I organized the April event with a Black lesbian focus at the Lesbian Herstory Archives (LHA) to recall what was in the archive. I made a zine to hand out so people could read along and follow along by decade and year, within the decade, what was going on. And I just pulled material from the collection. And so that was my second time gathering and putting my hands on Salsa Soul Sisters' material and transmitting it to an audience. It turns out that there was a considerable amount of Salsa Soul already in the collection from a previous LHA coordinator, Georgia Brooks, who also sat for some time as part of the Salsa Soul Sisters board of directors. She created a small Salsa collection of board minutes but also contributed images and clippings that were interspersed throughout the collection. Black lesbians, Georgia, and others, like Barbara Smith, Jewelle Gomez, and Irare Sabasu, to name a few, had always been active at LHA. I used the zine format to outline this herstory, and I also had women come and perform the zine interspersed throughout the room, and every time we would go to another page, it would be another year. And then somebody would stand up and personify the voice of the woman who, say, wrote the poem, or had written the essay, or had been just sort of narrating the piece that was presented for that year.

SM: I just have to go back to this planning discussion for these panels and the discussion that there were no Black lesbians in the seventies because that seems ridiculous given the context of the conference — centering lesbians!

SCC: The opinions were they were there, they just weren't doing anything.

SM: What do you make of that statement? Was it sarcastic, to say, because it hasn't been documented it doesn't exist?

SCC: No, it wasn't said in a critical way; it was said in an unfortunately evidential way. The only two Black lesbians in the room were me and a young woman who was a doctoral student at the CUNY Graduate Center in environmental psychology. She was not around in the seventies. We were both like, well, maybe they're right. I knew of Cheryl Clarke, Audre Lorde, and Barbara Smith, but I was tired of them being the people that everyone called upon — exhausted for them to be having to speak for an entire community at all times.

SM: Like tokens.

SCC: Exactly. And you know, under-appreciatively. So, like, are they going to get paid for this? How are they going to get compensated? Like, every five seconds, when someone needs a Black lesbian of the time, that's them. I figured I would do my best to be the coordinator of whatever would happen. I would go to LHA to determine if there might indeed be nothing to find. It turns out there was *so* much material that I was, like, laughing out loud. I had it all smattered across on the table — and in just one box of many.

So that's why I made the zine, because I felt the need for other people to see these materials in the same way, just, like, a smattering of clippings.

SM: So, when you came across that box of materials, what was that process like? As you picked out materials, were you discovering all-new herstory, or did you have specific people or events in mind?

SCC: I was looking for names of specific people and also discovering new material at the same time. I was looking to do a traditional panel, so I was focusing in on names, but then it turned into publications and organizations and experiences and themes that were appearing, some of which were surprising when you put the words "Black" and "lesbian" together. One example was women who were being "butched" because they were Black and not because they identified as a butch lesbian. There was this assumption that their race made them more masculine, and I've had that experience. I'm all about being a femme, whether or not it's obvious, but I have had people make this assumption about me, too.

I went to a Fire & Ink Conference in 2009 at the University of Texas, which was a convening for Black LGBT writers, and they put the speaker photos in the back of the program. I did a presentation on grants, research, and writing, so my photo was in there. At the end of the conference, I walked up to someone and asked, "Oh, how did you like it?" And they were like, "Oh, I thought the conference is great. But I really wish that I met this one person." And I was like, "Oh, who is it?"

SM: It was you!

SSC: And there were, like, four women having this conversation together. And then one of them goes to the back of the program, and they're all collectively like, "Oh yeah, she's so hot. I wish I would have met her." It's me! I'm standing right in front of them, and they didn't know it was me.

SM: [laughs and groans] Wow, did you eventually key them in?

SCC: Yeah, I told them it was me, and they were just so disappointed. I call that my butch photo, which I have used, and it has gotten me far. So, it's true that there is a butching that happens in the Black lesbian community. Yet, that was a photo. It definitely happens almost always in any version of interracial dating I've experienced. White lesbians that I've dated have all except once (and I've dated a lot of white women in my twenties) assumed I would take on the masculine role. I dated femme white women so as not to have to perform the dichotomized role-play, but it always backfired. In their defense, I can be very handsome, and do have these Jamaican muscles, and there is a part of me that hardens around femininity that I am attracted to, so…

Going back to the event I did at LHA with the zine I made, I thought maybe twenty-five people would come because I do events with LHA all the time. Over a hundred people came! I know because I made eighty copies of the zine, and we were well out of copies. People were sitting on the steps. People were arriving after the fact. I mean, it was like people were piling on top of each other. And a lot of the women were women from the time who came, so a lot of elder-dykes came. And by the end, once we got past seventy-five people, people started volunteering to read parts in the zine, to voice the sounds of the letters. We also had audio and video going, so there were other components to how people were experiencing the seventies at that time.

SM: Were they reading their own parts?

SCC: No, they were sort of like, "I came out to this" or, "I recall this journal of *Conditions*, issue five, the Black issue." That was sort of a landmark issue because it had national distribution, and the editors, Lorraine Bethel and Barbara Smith, were guest editors, and Elly Bulkin was on the *Conditions* collective. There had been Black lesbians featured throughout the journal's history, but that was, like, *the* Black lesbian — or, the Black woman's issue, 'cause, you know, it was too soon to be "L" wording it.

Ultimately, at that LHA event, I made a lot of connections. In the fall panel — that was also a Black lesbian panel — Imani Rashid, who is one of the Salsa Soul folks, was put on the panel — "we" meaning Alexis Pauline Gumbs — who's a well-known Black lesbian scholar who has done the mobile homecoming project — she and her partner, Sangodare. Alexis was on the final panel along with a South African intern who had worked with GALA, now named Jabu Pereira, an archivist. Although we were reading material from people of Salsa Soul and they were a part of the seventies outline, it was sort of like one of many things. But this LHA exhibit, event, and the zine I put together ended up being printed hundreds of times over. It traveled the country with a people of color zine tour with the POC Zine Project.

A few things would continue to happen throughout the years in relation to the Salsa Soul Sisters archive and my involvement in it. By 2013, I got platonically married, and we had a huge wedding at Imani's house in the Hamptons. Imani is one of the people that was on the board of Salsa Soul, and the wedding had a group of lesbians that were there to help perform the wedding — cook and serve the food, perform, and a DJ. Imani's friends came, and they were also Salsa Soul Sisters women.

This formal community meeting and conversations about history with the CLAGS conference turned into personal experiences and sharing family and witnessing life, all certain moments. I wrote about it in *Sinister Wisdom* 118, which pays homage to the Lesbian Herstory Archives turning 45. So, all of this sort of converged. That weekend allowed the trust to be gained for them to finally agree to have their collection sent to the LHA archives.

By 2016, I did a keynote at the LGBT ALMS conference (Archivists, Librarians, Museums, and Special Collections conference) in London on Salsa Soul Sisters as a current under-exposed and under-appreciated resource — but also about this hidden narrative of conflict that I find within lesbian of color communities. There tend to be issues with secrecy or distrust in general. And the distrust leads some people's stories to not be told because they end up not giving their materials to places that would preserve them. I compared it with Rivers of Honey, the cabaret that I helped to produce, in that we had parallel issues where there was mistrust, infighting, and as a result, hurt feelings and lost friendships.

SM: Let's pause and trace the transfer. We start with you finding out about the Salsa Soul Sisters through the ALUSCC panel. You then begin research for the panel event and programming you're working on at LHA archives, and you're going through things, and they happen to be a part of your selected materials?

SSC: Well, the through-line is they were no longer just artifacts or documents — they were people. I'm sure I appreciated their work prior to that as well. But it was when I made eyes with them, broke bread with them, and constantly interacted with them in the community. In fact, a lot of the women who were doing SSS then are still active. They're currently doing LGBT Kwanzaa in New York. I've been to and performed at the Kwanzaa. Learning about their history — like, you're in a room full of elder dykes and they start telling you stories about back in the day and suddenly you really get a sense of what they were experiencing and where, what it was about, and what kind of spaces they were inhabiting, and what that must have been like. So, it's really about them being active and seeking out community still and working with women who are younger than them and passing it on and wanting to tell their stories.

The LHA event was a way for them to learn about me and know that I was connected to the archives. One of the women who I chose as a player for the zine performances is Kaz Mitchell, and I interviewed her partner, the late Jean Wimberly, for the Michigan Women's Music Festival issue of *Sinister Wisdom* 103 because she was one of the women who started the women of color tent there. Do you know about Michfest?

SSC: I do, and I've read that piece that you're talking about, but I never had a chance to go myself.

SSC: I was a Festie, and I think that the mission of the Michigan Women's Music Festival changed my life and really got me to understand the impact of the intergenerational nature of the community, its culture, and the longevity of it. Michfest was also around from the seventies until now, or until then. The women of color tent there — there was nothing like it in the world. It was this magical possibility. Jean Wimberly was also a member of Salsa Soul, and she talks about how when she came to New York from Philadelphia, when she was just a young 20-something, she walked right into Salsa and that was sort of her connecting point to a community. And she had a van and would take women to Michfest. So, just the way that transferred on from everybody's individual story really did create community in different ways — those who are still around wanting to tell their stories.

In 2016, there was the keynote and the actual donation. So, it was that November that Cassandra Grant, Imani Rashid, Nancy Valentine, and Brahma Curry brought their objects to the archives as the official Salsa Soul Sisters organization donation. It could've been a typical donation process — say, for example, putting it in the mail and I could just receive it, send them a letter thanking them. But this was so ceremonious: we had catering and we poured libations and there were speeches and it was recorded.

SM: It was a celebration!

SSC: It was! I remember talking to Steven Fullwood, who started the Black LGBT archive at the Schomburg, about the experience of the SSS donation. And he says, you know, that's perfect — that's how it should *always* be. Whenever someone donates their materials into an archive, it should be a celebration, and it should be a recognition of that moment of transferring their material to this other place that's going to keep it and hold it. Having said that, I'm a bit critical of archives because when you put something in an archive, it's sort of like a back closet and leaving it for the devices of archivists to be cataloged. Depending on the resources of the organization, that's how detailed the cataloguing will be.

SM: It's sort of like a holding place.

SSC: Right! It's not a guarantee of some immortalizing force. I felt like the response from the donors was, "So now what, where's our website?"

SM: They expected instant engagement and public presence.

SSC: Absolutely. I wanted to be sensitive to that because they were distrustful in general about giving their material to an archive. I didn't want them to feel like, well, we gave it to the LHA and then they didn't do anything with it.

SM: Sure. You wanted to be good stewards.

SSC: Right. And so I said, well, it's not really the task of the archive to do something with it, at that intermediary point. When you go to library school and you learn archiving, you don't learn about exhibitions. They do more so nowadays. It's about access to the material as soon as possible. But initially, when I was in library school, you learned about preservation, and that was pretty much it. Like, here's how to put it in an HVAC facility. Here's how to catalog it and make it discoverable when it's sought after, but not here's how to get a grant to make an exhibition. It doesn't happen without resources and a staff. At LHA, we do have a collaboration with the Pratt School of Library Science where the students, throughout a course, will process an archive and they'll put it online, but that's full-time students who are using this to get employed after and they have the energy of students who are paying, who knows what, $40,000 a semester to go to Pratt. It's not like a volunteer who's once a week coming in and spending two hours. There's a very different power behind that. We also contract with Gale Cengage to have digitized some of our collections and have them accessible via their online database, but this is a closed resource for institutions who can afford access. And even still, this is item-focused, keyword searching, which is very different from a Salsa Soul Sisters website.

So, all of that is to say, I did want to respond to their interest, and that's why we agreed to do an exhibition.

SM: And this was in 2016?

SSC: Yes, and then, of course, like, they donated it in November, but in October, I found out that I was pregnant after trying for three years, so then everything had to be on hold. My pregnancy wasn't easy. Even now, my baby's turning one, and I'm like, okay, I have to do this exhibition, but I got to come home and breastfeed. I'm not the same person that I was in 2010 when I did a program that one hundred people came to.

The reason why the exhibition was able to happen is due to a few reasons. The archives had just recently done exhibitions. There was a relationship with the gallery for which we had the exhibit that was pre-coordinated by an LHA Graphics committee. Some backstory on the Graphics Committee and any conversation about LHA exhibitions has to acknowledge that though many of the LHA coordinators are activists, or are librarians, one of our coordinators has a doctorate in art history and is also a pioneer in lesbian art activism, Dr. Flavia Rando. In 2006, I discovered LHA through a class at Brooklyn College, "The Lesbian Experience," that I petitioned to take and have kept in the women's studies department, taught by Flavia Rando, one of the original Radical Lesbians, which is one of the first radical lesbian organizations. In the syllabus, she put in a tour of the LHA. I was completely overcome. I still remember that tour. I went to the second floor room. I opened Audre Lorde's box, and I swear, I heard angels sing, you know, like, there was light coming from it.

It totally changed my life, and this course ended up having the highest enrollment in the women's studies department's history. And, in the ten years since they had taken it off and after three semesters of it, they changed the title to "The Women's Experience." They took out lesbian. When they offered it in 2006, after not giving it for ten years, every class had new people attending, sitting on the floor. It was packed. The course ended up taking the space of a support group. It was people coming out in real space with real people. It was therapy. It was activism. It was real learning.

SM: What's up with the name change?

SSC: I would say it was a homophobic move on the part of the women's studies department chair at the time. Flavia ended up leaving. There were legal ramifications. I mean, there was, like, a big thing surrounding this course.

SM: I imagine they tried to couch it within an enrollment argument.

SSC: One thing I know is people were concerned about putting lesbian on their transcripts. That was a valid concern. There was too much attention paid to the course and the school wasn't comfortable with that kind of attention. At the end of the day, Brooklyn College is a very conservative CUNY school. It had a lot of money from its Hillel house and from the Jewish alumni, it's a lot of private funding into that college, and they really just had to follow the money. So, Flavia ended up taking her course to LHA.

SM: Oh, wow.

SSC: I think it's in the sixth or seventh year she started the Lesbian Studies Institute, and every semester she teaches "The Lesbian Experience" at the archives. It's a ten-week course and has full enrollment every semester. She uses the archive for the course, as the course. And the course is going through the collection. I interview Flavia in a similar vein as this interview for *Sinister Wisdom* 118: *Forty-Five Years / Celebrating the Lesbian Herstory Archives*.

So, Flavia with her art history background, she became a coordinator of the archives, and she also helped to do some exhibitions. We worked on an exhibition with the Elizabeth Foundation for the Arts Robert Blackburn Printmaking Workshop, and because the gallery is also a printmaking workshop, I was asked to be a zine resident. I pitched the idea of the SSS exhibition as I was still processing this collection. I have a meeting once a month with a volunteer, Stahimili Mapp, a Black lesbian elder-dyke, to process it, but I knew they wanted it more than just labeled boxes. I decided that I would make my zine residency the SSS zine.

It was through the making of a zine, in the same way that it had been in 2010, that this other thing came about.

SM: What do you think is notable about the zine format?

SSC: People are excited about zines because they're sort of like an art book, and they're easily transferable. The format is easy to produce and inexpensive to replicate. There's still something about it that's a little bit underground, a little bit retro, and bad ass — rather than, say, a chapbook, which is very formal.

SM: And editioned, usually. There are rules.

SSC: Yeah, exactly. A zine can be whatever you want it to be. That makes people excited about it. And you don't know what it is going to be until you see it.

The zine for the Salsa Soul Sisters exhibition is meant to unveil itself at the exhibition. I think part of what the zine will become is not a comprehensive biography of the group but about my story and process exhibiting them. Somehow, it's going to incorporate the conversation of getting it into the archive.

SM: What are some of the objects from the collection that you're including and some of the more personal moments? Are there photos from your wedding?

SSC: Salsa was a very social group — summer excursions, dances, consciousness-raising groups, and discussion sessions — so we're going to have flyers from each of those to represent the fact that they met every Thursday and had an agenda and a calendar. I'm working on trying to get a map made that had points for where they met in the city. I think that maps are fun to locate us in space and time. They'll have the coordinates on the map and say they met in the Bronx and in Brooklyn, but they were also often in the West Village, and part of what they wanted to do was to buy a building, and that never happened. It always boils down to space and access to space in New York City. Had they bought that building, you know, what would be different now in terms of culture and lesbian narrative?

SM: And would the archive have been transferred to you or would the archive be living, still being made?

SSC: Right! We're going to have an altar with obituary cards from women who have passed.

SM: Is the altar going to be Black women in the lesbian community?

SSC: I think it's supposed to be SSS members, but it's possible that it could be people's friends. I think that would be expected because we're going to have a panel in the middle of it. I feel like the exhibit can shift and move and bend depending on who's in the room and what they want to add to it. We do want to give people the opportunity to donate their materials to the archives. We'll share what was donated, and then hopefully it encourages people to share materials they might want to preserve.

SM: Transfer your materials to this archive so that we can continue to build it. Would that be your vision for the show and the way that people are going to experience it — to come and maybe leave something behind?

SSC: We don't think that's a good idea because you don't want things to get lost, but we do want it to be a reconnection for those who have been like, those were still around. I mean, since 2010, when we did the original talk at the archives, so many women have passed in the past eight years, you know, as they would have, and so we want it to be another place for them to see each other and go out and have an evening of seeing their friends. We also want to attract the younger crowd of people who haven't heard of SSS before, who can in some ways find some new meaning in what they already do.

SM: So, the concept of transfer is in every single aspect of this — programming, exhibition, and the impetus for the whole thing.

SSC: As a community archivist, I see archiving as no other way than in the continuous exchange of narratives, the respect, and receipt of our lives. An honoring.

THINGS I LOST AT Q BAR

Nomi F. Beesen

(San Francisco circa 2009)

A grey hooded sweatshirt
A blue-green 2-gauge plastic earring
My wallet (later found)
My drink
My inhibitions
An adjustable wrench
My dignity
The next day
A book of Gary Snyder poetry
That lovin feeling (later found)
A black woolen hat
My nerve
My chance
A girl

THINGS I LOOKED FOR AT METROPOLITAN BAR

Nomi F. Beesen

(Brooklyn circa 2013)

Love
The bartender's attention
A cigarette
Trouble
A woman
A hot dog
A way to forget (oblivion)
A way to hold the bathroom door shut while peeing
My roommate
A Siouxsie and the Banshees dance party
Inspiration (a woman)
A place to make out
A reason to stay in NYC
Belonging

Nomi F. Beesen is a recent transplant from Brooklyn to the Hudson Valley, where they are still getting used to country living (there was a bear in the backyard last month) and so much enjoying the trees and air. So much. But Nomi's heart is scattered in various places, among them Seattle, SF Bay Area, Provincetown, and, most of all, Brooklyn, where many of their dearest ones live. What is home anyway, and where is the queer bar? Nomi is a book editor and writes and draws/paints when the call comes. Lots of their time is spent slowing down and opening up to that call. www.nomibeesen.com

ON NONLINEAR JOURNEYS AND ADVOCATING FOR YOURSELF AND OTHERS

A conversation with Camila Coddou, founder of Barista Behind the Bar

Camila Coddou (she/her) is a QWOC currently living and working on the traditional Chinook lands (Portland, OR). Founder of The Pause Project—a month-long workshop about slowing down and connecting with yourself—she is passionate about writing, employee rights, and being an Aries. When she isn't writing, she can be found with an oat milk latte in hand walking her miniature poodle mix, Bruiser. Find her online at sistersundown.com and on IG @sister_sundown and @baristabehindthebar.

SM: I really appreciate you taking some time to talk with me. I started this project in 2017, when I was in between jobs, pivoting career-wise, and had recently discovered *Sinister Wisdom* — was excited to get involved however I could. I started the Instagram account because I felt people should know about this. I follow accounts for the Lesbian Herstory Archives, and, as problematic as social media is, I think that presence can also serve a crucial connective purpose and provide access into a shared history that isn't being taught for marginalized subcultures and communities.

The whole concept of transfer. I was thinking about it a lot as I was in this extended moment of transition between working full-time in the art world and all the unlearning that I was starting to do around toxic habits and behaviors that I was taught to practice and reinforce as a curator and as an arts programmer and was then hearing about how Julie (*Sinister Wisdom's* editor) had just moved the *Sinister Wisdom* archives from the Bay Area to Florida, and I started to think: What are ways that I, and we, can, disrupt transferring what no longer serves us? How do we shift gears?

When I found out about the Barista Behind the Bar project — an interview series to engage in conversation with baristas who have worked in the specialty coffee industry in the United States about their experience — it resonated with me because sometimes you get put in a situation that's awful and unfair and it tests you and your sense of self and your ability to take a risk, right? To speak up and speak out. You made the decision to advocate for an equitable, healthy work environment for yourself and the employees you managed and challenged a former employer — resulting in you leaving the coffee shop and a catalyst for Barista Behind the Bar. And I've been there and in different ways, of course. I have a lot of privilege as a white, cis-gendered woman, but no matter how outspoken you are, the question of "What is this going to mean for me? Will I lose my job? Am I going to lose my professional standing?" We've seen time and again what people lose. Returning to the connection potential of social media, I started following Barista Behind the Bar and was so impressed by how you turned what was a personal hardship into something that could raise awareness for the way you were treated and the way that other people are treated in the coffee industry.

CC: Well, thank you. I appreciate you saying so!

SM: I remember being struck by how comfortable people, especially now, are with being openly awful. I wanted to get some more context from you on what happened. What was the turning point for you to know you needed to say something?

CC: Sure. So, I worked for a company for five years, mostly in upper-level management. When I was hired, I was one of only about two people of color on a staff of around thirty. There were no Black people on staff at all. In the five years that I spent with them, I made it my work to bring equity, inclusion, and diversity into not just the visible company culture, but, like, the backend operational ethos. That work is obviously worldly, but it's also deeply personal, you know — a queer woman of color on a team that's homogenous within an industry that is classically run by cis white dudes. It's a tall order, and it's also quite personal, to the point that it's emotionally draining. Once you're doing that work, then it's so personal, and you realize how quickly you need to learn to walk the fine line between making progress and utter exhaustion at your personal expense. Added to that conversation is asking yourself if the people you're working for are interested in engaging in this work and learning, or are you barking up the wrong damn tree?

SM: Yes. Something that came out in some of the interviews that I read that you've done with BBB, is that sometimes you don't know what side they're on, so to speak, until you're really in deep and invested.

CC: Well, basically in that time, in those five years, my method was to sort of work behind the scenes. I saw a change that needed to happen. I felt empowered enough; I had their trust. So, I feel empowered enough by ownership to hire with diversity in mind and to create a training program that would invite people in who are traditionally gate-kept out of the industry. That became my ethos, kind of flying under the radar, doing what I had to get done. And then also, like, subverting the whole thing but still doing it within the safety, comfort, and support of ownership. What I learned through that experience, and this is something I speak about with baristas and management on a regular basis, is knowing when you're on your own and when the work isn't worth it. If you are not an owner, you need to consider your labor and what you're bringing to the table and whether or not it's ultimately worth your time.

SM: That part is so important. Now that I'm more in the corporate world in the work that I do as a managing editor, I think about leadership support. In my prior job, and as an ERG lead while there, that was always the crux of our frustrations: that the business doesn't actually want to follow up on topics of a panel discussion on how to broaden your recruitment strategy. They don't actually want to do that work — they just want us to do it, for free, on top of (and not as an integral, recognized part) of our jobs.

CC: As a general manager, the relationship for me with that company felt extremely fulfilling on a day-to-day basis when I was working directly with employees because I was in charge of hiring and training all retail staff. However, what ended up happening to me is what happens so often for people in that position — you end up positioning yourself between the shit that is rolling downhill and the people who you manage that deserve better. For me, it's historical; that's the role I play in my family. I am the keeper of garbage. And I'm like, I know all the information. I'm going to do my best to keep you safe. I'm going to do my best to make sure employees I know get that safety and peace, all the while knowing that the powers that be — in this case, the owners of the coffee company I used to manage — are not actually interested in that work.

This dynamic became a breaking point. The more that I, like, dug my heels into advocating for employee needs and rights, the more I found myself to be at odds with ownership — and the more they tried to push me out. That I essentially worked for this company for five years, gave it my all, and we weren't always on the same page — that's totally fine. But I was the general manager, and I had a lot of power. I had a lot of projects in the air. I was in charge of a lot of people. When I put in my two weeks' notice in October 2018 — I'll never forget this — on a Thursday night, I emailed both owners and said I believed our time together had come to an end and that I wanted this to be a seamless transition. I mentioned that I was giving two weeks, but that I could be available to discuss staying on longer should you need to hire someone to replace, whatever.

SM: That sounds super gracious and really generous.

CC: I sent that email, and the very next day, I woke up to an email from the main owner saying, "Today's your last day; your check will be ready at noon. Return your keys."

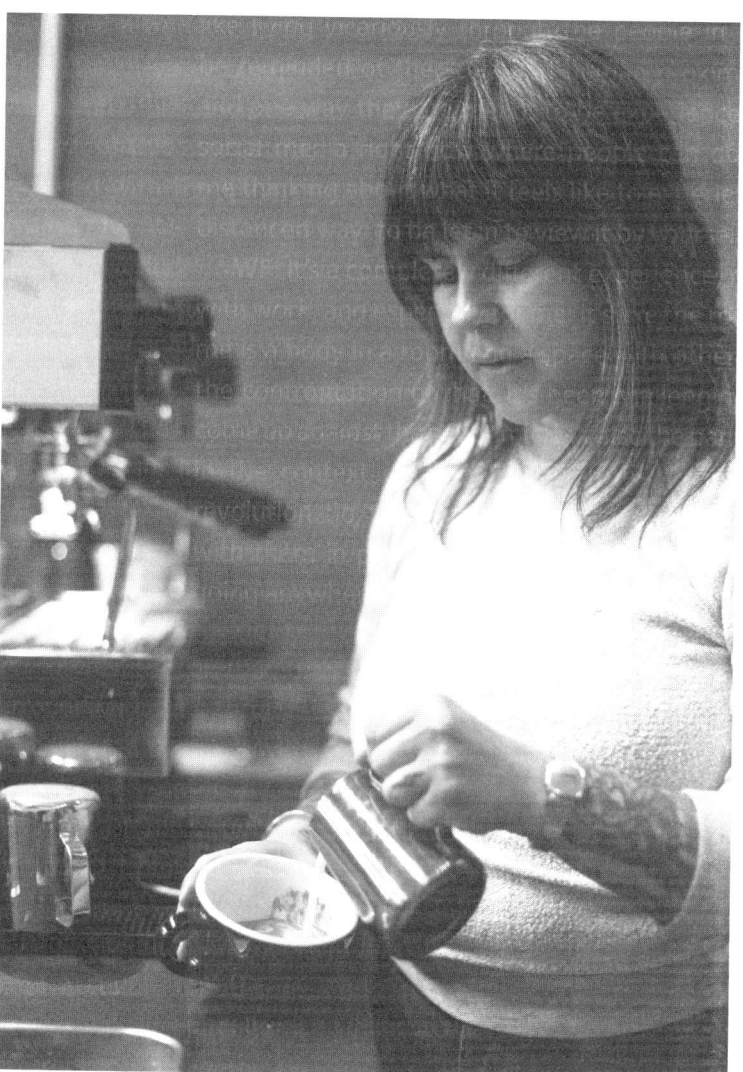

Camila Coddou

SM: Wow. Like, don't let the door hit you on the way out, essentially.

CC: Yep. Literally, thank you for nothing. I mean, that is just like rude as fuck, but even just from a self-preservation standpoint, I do not understand why you would leave all your current staff without leadership, without management. That really set the stage for then when there was a huge PR nightmare, which happened soon after I quit, around one of the owners' YouTube series in which they questioned the accounts of assault survivors. When that happened, staff didn't have direct leadership. They had no one to turn to be like, "Whoa, this is problematic" or, "Oh my God, customers are coming in and yelling at us for this video." Or like, when the Proud Boys [a far-right and neo-fascist, male-only organization that promotes and engages in political violence in the United States and Canada] are filtering into our cafes — how do we handle this? There was no one in place to support them because that would have been my job and they didn't hire anybody to replace me.

SM: So, the timeline of events is: you gave your notice to the coffee shop, which they handled poorly and showed no interest in a smooth transition despite you having offered. And then, the YouTube video stuff happened. You quitting and those videos by one of the owners of that coffee shop are separate incidents, but you got involved because you were seeing your former staff completely left in the dust to fend for themselves because of the direct actions of the owner who made the videos.

CC: Right, exactly. How I came to be involved with the entire fallout of the YouTube series circus is that I saw the video and thought, this is not appropriate. This is not okay. So, I posted something about it on my social media, and it kinda fucking blew up from there. I didn't expect that to happen. But to me, that's just indicative of the fact that the staff who were there were at a loss with what to do, and because I was the last person in that position of leadership and we had built trust over, like, half a decade together, I kind of assumed that role. The conversation reaches beyond the cafe, you know. It was a tipping point in our culture.

I wasn't involved with the shop anymore, and I wasn't beholden to them for a paycheck, so I helped some current and former staff mobilize to put out a public statement and get in touch with local media. The information was already out there; the person who put those videos out and the people that appear in the videos are well-known, published authors. Like, this wasn't a thing we uncovered. It was a public. They wanted people to see it and have a reaction.

SM: Well, thank you for going back into that experience. I know it's hard — when I've had to retell my version of that experience, it's very emotional.

CC: I've definitely had a lot of time to contextualize and sit with what happened, but yes, it's a lot!

SM: So, as you're advocating for your former colleagues, empowering them with tools, resources, and support to handle that situation, where does Barista Behind the Bar come into play? Did you think, "I've had this idea and like, like, why not now?" Was there any other catalysts there that you think people should know about in terms of how the project came to be?

CC: It was a huge period of transition. I had just ended my most significant professional relationship, which, aside from the hardship, was also incredibly important to me. That was one huge change. And that was a relationship that I needed to grieve, but that I wasn't given the time and space to appropriately grieve it. Then the YouTube stuff came out, and I threw myself into that. Somewhere in there during this time, my father, who had been struggling with cancer, passed away within a few days of the YouTube stuff unfolding. So, all of this transition, change, and this crazy energy. And in all of that, I felt pretty groundless. Here I am, I have all this experience working in the coffee industry, but I questioned whether it was something I wanted to continue doing. I had just lost my father and was thinking about what to do next. In moments like that, I thought, I would love it if I could take some time to myself and go on a trip. Leave my normal life just for, like, a minute and recharge, but I wondered, how do I finance that? Social media plays such a funny role in this because when I was involved with the YouTube situation, I made all of these amazing new coffee friends from around the country. Wouldn't it be cool if I took a road trip, met some of the people that I got to know through that experience? Maybe pick up some guest shifts here and there or learn about different coffee shops?

It snowballed from there. People are following my personal page because they were interested in the circle that I had and the fight that I had with my former employer and are reaching out to me sharing stories of similar things that have happened to them — and that they didn't receive support. I started noticing this pattern in those interactions. Over the course of a shower and a subsequent conversation with my partner, I thought, what if I go on a trip? What if I finance it by working guest shifts wherever I land? And then I considered that, while I'm speaking with baristas on these guest shifts, I could also talk with them about their experiences. What if we could have a collective, national conversation about what it's like to feel supported in your place of work?

SM: Kudos to you navigating that time and deciding to go for it and pour yourself into the Barista Behind the Bar project. I can definitely relate. There's a tendency when you are going through a significant hardship or sadness like that for it to be spun as such a generative, creative time. I think this idea gets romanticized, especially in the art world — turn your trauma into art. But I also think that it can be a generative period because you're in this raw state where you're reassessing everything.

CC: Absolutely.

SM: It's so cool that you were able to channel a little bit of that challenging time into taking care of yourself and other people. On the topic of taking care of yourself and other people, talk me through that initial travel element. I remember from your posts on Instagram that you were going to get a van and built that out so you could live in there and travel around. What was that process like? How were you thinking about the process of traveling then as both a practical function to earn some money and to grow the BBB project, and how are you thinking about travel and transfer now? What's different about the conversation we're having now over the phone and being there in the coffee shop or the place where people are working?

Camila Coddou

Photo Credit: Camila Coddou

CC: I ended up pivoting pretty quickly from the idea of working guest shifts in addition to interviewing baristas because it became pretty clear to me that if I'm immersing myself in the culture of a coffee shop and then also interviewing people about potential hardships at that cafe or roastery, there was going to be a conflict of interest. So, I moved away from that model and instead raised the money through finding sponsorship. The travel element, rather than going and visiting coffee shops to work, it was more about let me meet you in your space. I also firmly believe in coffee shops as a third space and how they reflect the community or not. I'm interested in the conversation around how you invite a community in, especially if you're a gentrifying force. How can you ameliorate that and support staff if you are hiring people from within the community? So, it became a reconnaissance mission to explore how other coffee shops are doing things elsewhere. How does it look to work in coffee in Cincinnati, Ohio? Or St. Louis, Missouri? Chicago or Durham? How do all these places handle those specific challenges, which seem to be ubiquitous, but, of course, will differ from community to community?

When I started, I was going to schedule four interviews a day, back-to-back. What I learned very quickly, which I'm sure you can understand as somebody who interviews people, is that when you're creating a vulnerable space with someone, it can be really exhausting. You're not interviewing folks about their favorite musician; you're interviewing them about emotional topics like how comfortable, supported, seen, and heard they feel in their workplace. To be the person who's asking people to share that information, it's imperative that I, in many ways, share my story to create that safe, shared space. I quickly realized I could only do three interviews in a day. I needed an hour between each one. I needed water and food.

One part of this project was being in community and having a conversation in the barista's preferred space because I want them to feel comfortable. A lot of times, we would not meet where they work, but in neutral places: a different coffee shop, the place where the friend worked, or a park. Meeting in-person and in that way creates a different space for vulnerability and support than over the phone or on Zoom.

SM: That's so important. I'm thinking about the way that we interview for coffee shop jobs, too. I remember when I interviewed for front of the house at Tartine, and you went up this winding staircase and into what felt like a crawl space [laughter]. I'm sure there's been some behavioral study on the way that people mimic and conform to the behavior of the interviewer when you are the interviewee. I think that's really key, that you paid attention to the environment for the conversations. What were some of the main themes that came up around how to tell the story? Did people have concerns? Did you find that people were worried about what would happen or how the story would live in the world?

CC: That was a huge consideration because the way that people speak, candidly, they're going to say what they feel and reference names, places, specific situations. When I interviewed everyone, I said speak to me candidly, and I will omit the business name everywhere. In that way, people could feel free to engage in a more stream-of-consciousness conversational moment. I would do a little bit of research into the person I was interviewing, but they were self-selected.

By the time I left Portland on this trip, I had almost 2,000 followers on the Barista Behind the Bar account (@baristabehindthebar) from all over the country. If you're interested in telling me your story, I'm interested in hearing it. I think that it's, of course, specific that the person who's asking to hear the stories is a woman of color. I doubt that as many people would feel as comfortable if I were a white dude. It's no coincidence that I'm the person who is putting myself in a spot and also creating that safety.

And then from there I might poke around on their Instagram and be like, Oh cool. Like, you know, you work for a bigger company, or you worked for more of a mom and pop shop, but really the interview was just a conversation. I would start with a few basics. I ask everybody what their favorite album to play at work is. And then from there it was just, you know, tell me whatever it is you want to talk about.

SM: I was just thinking about the music I listened to when I worked at Tartine and how contentious it got in there between the customers and workers. I have to hand it to the managers though, you could listen to whatever the fuck you wanted. People would openly complain about the music. *Jagged Little Pill* — my music of choice — got so many complaints! The Mission District in San Francisco [the location of the original Tartine Bakery] changed so much, even in the time — I only worked there two and a half years, and it was so different. The folks that would roll through changed from, like, this eclectic clientele of musicians, artists, and Andrew who owned Adobe Bookstore, you know, and then it became, give me this food, let me take a photo of it. And also, no one tipped. When people who come in who obviously haven't worked in service, it's obvious.

There is a great quote on the website: "When you create a welcoming place of employment, you by extension create community spaces where clientele feel welcomed, where people feel good." What was so important to you when you were in that general manager role, and in general now — and I don't know if you want to go back to work in coffee ever, in the same way — but with diversity, equity, and inclusion becoming such a mainstream topic now, it's forcing people to go beyond virtue signaling. People will find the receipts. They are going to dig and know if you posted a black square and then turned around and donated to the Trump campaign. Your actions need to meet your words. In the context of the interviews you've been doing, how have their work experiences changed after talking with you and the interview going live? You were focused on developing these relationships as well, so I don't know if you keep in touch with everyone, but I'm curious about that ecosystem.

CC: That's a really good question. The project as an enterprise has evolved. Initially it was heavy on documentation of stories. Am I a journalist and do I want all the information, or am I looking through the lens of inequity and abuse? Invariably people who are having a good time are less apt to talk about it. The interview structure began primarily as archival methodology. It has moved from this journalistic collection and representation to more of a robust network system on Instagram almost exclusively. It has also turned into more of an on-the-ground, community event-based support system. I do not get the sense that people's jobs are getting better just yet.

As a society, we're in the period of listening. We're not in the period of change yet. People are making change, but the change that is made without sustainability is not going to stick. If you can't as an employee rely on health insurance, who gives a shit if you don't play the music you want to play? The conversation needs to move beyond surface level. The conversations that I'm having are continuations of a similar theme: everybody's experience is unique and also inequity is systemic across the coffee industry and every industry. The stories that I'm hearing right now are digging further in and being like, "Wow, that thing that happened to me that one time is rooted in this much bigger problem."

I don't believe that people's on-the-ground work realities are changing *just* yet. But I do believe that we're finally having the conversations that we need to be having in order for anything to actually change.

SM: Certainly, what the pandemic has done to, like, the global economy and the American economy, the priority now is just keep your job. People don't feel necessarily empowered to advocate for themselves beyond that. They're worried about paying their bills.

I want to go back to what you said about this period of listening because as someone who's studied a lot of history, I wouldn't say I'm a cynic, but I definitely see a lot of patterns here. I talk with people that are just joining the conversation around systemic inequity and white supremacist capitalism who say they had no idea it was this bad. It's always been an issue; we're just being forced to pay attention to it right now. Humanity is slow to change. I'm encouraged by, for example, what seems like is happening in Minneapolis around the protests for justice for George Floyd. My last arts job and the one where I got fired from for advocating for myself and for other folks at the museum. There were news articles about it. It was fucking terrible. I was curating shows with queer artists and artists of color. That conversation was still so new there. I'm encouraged to see that the protests have at least led to a period of listening. The city of Minneapolis is committing to thinking about how to utilize resources in a different way and defunding the police. I'm curious on the barista and coffee industry level what you're seeing in terms of this period of listening. Are things coming up that are unexpected or that are emerging about access, inclusion, disrupting the status quo, you could say, like, within that industry?

CC: Yes and no. As always, the people who are screaming the loudest are the ones with the least amount of political power and financial clout, and the people who are comfortable with their life aren't as much. In some ways, it's heartening that more people are turning around and listening. But on the other hand, people are mad and exhausted. The reason that I feel like we're in a listening place is because you can't sweep people's completely legitimate feelings and exhaustion under the rug. It's not enough to acknowledge that you haven't been listening. There needs to be a period of reckoning and apology. If you hurt someone, you make space for people to feel their legitimate feelings. And that's never happened because it doesn't fit into the capitalist structure of finance. Now, against the backdrop of the coronavirus, so many of us aren't working and are resting as best we can now. And we are talking about self-care. We know now that most of our jobs can be done from home, and we're pulling the curtain back to reveal the truth, and I do think that correlation is making for a more potent conversation.

SM: This feeds into how we're groomed to behave in these circumstances. It's considered unprofessional to be honest about what happened to you in an interview context. You're never supposed to speak ill of your former employer or the people you worked with or the way that you were retreated.

CC: You're not encouraged to speak truth to any sort of emotion that you may or not have on the clock because in capitalism, time is money. You can't monetize someone's emotional reaction. I ran into this a lot at my former workplace; wanting acknowledgement was seen as weak — like, what do you need me to acknowledge you for? You're getting a paycheck. A feminist workplace is a place that makes space for people to have the actual emotions that they're already having and to make that part of the job, part of the work. We're not encouraged to have that, but that is deeply unhealthy.

SM: What advice would you give to people who are, like, in those situations where they want to speak up, but they're not really sure where to start, and they're dealing with all the intersections of privilege, race, class, and access?

CC: The ability to speak up is steeped in privilege. You need to have a certain amount of access or financial backing from family or a partner to be able to feel like you could be safe enough. My advice is to do what you need for you. Speaking up, especially if you are a member of a marginalized group, sometimes the biggest action you can do is to leave. Make a lateral move if you have to. A lot of times people don't want to leave a job for a similar job elsewhere. But in the coffee industry, people are willing to make lateral moves in exchange for better company culture. That understood mobility within our industry positions people to be able to, like, seek employment in a place that, literally, the only thing that is different is that they feel more safe or better represented in their staffing or upper-level management. Removing yourself from a place that doesn't feel good if you don't feel like you can speak up is a huge act of resistance. In terms of speaking up and feeling safe and creating a safe space for someone to do that, I think it's important to speak with other people on your team and see if anybody else is having similar or analogous experiences and like, you know, see, see if there's, like, a support system that you can create from allyship. Silence is violence. It's bad business to turn away from that if you're an employer, and if you're an employer and ten people quit, you can turn away from that, but at what cost to your business? Customers notice when there's huge turnover.

Doing this work in particular, I kind of laugh because people will come to Portland and ask, where they should get coffee? And I'm like, I know too much about the shitty business practices.

What I tell people, and this is my metric, is to support the barista. Go to a place where you care about who's behind the counter. You will never 100% know about the ownership. Support the people who work day in and day out, who you care about. Tip them. That's the work.

Photo Credit: Kale Chesney

Camila Coddou

SM: In my last job, I led our queer employee resource group, and I worked with our Black employee resource group there to bring in, um, Black-owned business. So like, our coffee service, for example, we brought in Red Day, um, which is based in Oakland, um, and we really tried to make that connection between, like, this is how you show up. Give them your business. Are there coffee shops that you admire?

CC: I've been in the coffee industry, mostly in management, for thirteen years. My main takeaway is business owners are imperfect people who happened to have more access than other people to start a business. When I think about the places I enjoy frequenting, these aren't places that I think have perfect practices or don't have work to do, but they are doing their best to listen. In Portland, since that's the scene I know the best, The Arrow Coffee Shop is great. It's not a roastery, but it is a local cafe and bakery, and they carry Deadstock, which is a Black-owned roastery in Portland. Junior's Roasted Coffee is another good option.

SM: Bringing it back to BBB, I enjoyed reading Joey's story, "The Honor of Service." There are so many lovely moments and anecdotes about what makes Joey's day special. You situate the reader so well, and I feel like I'm there. I am not a coffee expert, and I was not in the industry for *that* long, but it takes me there. I love the part about his signature service gesture, which was weighing each shot, no matter how busy it got. What's your signature service that you provide?

CC: It's funny because in my ten years of coffee, I don't consider myself a star barista. I trained people, for so many companies, on coffee, but for me, I've always considered myself management, and what that means for me and what it has meant behind the counter is the person-to-person component of coffee. Businesses are about people, but coffee is *so* much about people. Coffee is social. There's this huge value chain from seed to cup, and it involves so many hands. What I find unique and so important about coffee is the human interactions. When I was behind the counter, I got a kick out of every single personality that walked through the door and liked meeting them where they were at. If you're not having a good day, I'm not going to engage with you in a conversation about the fucking single origin. Or you've been here five times this week, and you're reading this huge book — what is that about? Realizing that I could have a conversation with almost every single person, at least who was interested in having a conversation like that — I feel like that was like my signature pieces, where you acknowledge that some people just want a coffee and want to go. Also, I should note that a lot of my coffee experience is in New York City, where a lot of people don't have time to talk [laughs].

SM: That's such a hallmark of any kind of customer service, meeting people where they are. You get to know regulars, too, in a particular way that feels special. Talk about care — you're taking care of hundreds of people each week. That's incredibly compassionate and empathetic to be able to switch like that.

CC: That is what I love so much about the interview with Joey is his unwavering commitment to hospitality. It's so labor-intensive. It's also seen as femme labor yet also so beautiful as a place of connection between two people in potentially completely different worlds who might never otherwise meet. What strikes me most is the importance of the position that all customer service employees hold, but also how crappy the rights are for minimum wage earners in those positions. No one gives a shit about the owners. It's about the person behind the bar and whether or not they made them feel good.

SM: Oh, yeah. I remember when healthy San Francisco kicked in, and I was working at Tartine, and people would look at the receipt and be like, "What's this charge?" And I'd say that's so I can have health insurance, like, shitty health insurance, but something. Some people were cool about it; others decided not to tip.

Let's talk about the next steps of the Barista Behind the Bar project. I was super excited to see this curriculum idea that you're developing. How can people find out more about supporting that and how will this document continue to live in the world?

CC: What is cool about Barista Behind the Bar is also what makes it incredibly challenging: it's just me. I have some financial support from industry partners. It's kind of overwhelming. It's a little exhausting. It feels like a bunch of responsibility, which is great. And, like, I asked for it for sure, but also, what's cool about it is that I get to pivot as much as I want. When it comes down to the curriculum, yes, I believe that it is ever-evolving and a living entity. It is not yet a document, but that is because there are so many documents out there, and I'm trying right now to remain incredibly nimble in terms of what completion and success look like.

ON MONUMENTS AND INVENTING OTHER BUILDING BLOCKS
— A conversation with artist Welly Fletcher

In reckoning with today's political, environmental, and social realities, sculptor **Welly Fletcher** creates objects that enact support. Fletcher builds their sculptures using visceral materials to communicate in body-based terms like weight, texture, temperature, scent, and sound reflection.

Her collaborative *Shields for Queer Kin* series employ interdependent materials and methods while exploring the diagonal as a literal manifestation of queer politics: leaning material-bodies form a sculptural field of resistance to the straight, right angles of the normative world. Fletcher sees the expanded field of sculpture as offering an increasingly rare opportunity for an embodied, intersectional, poetic experience of otherness.

Fletcher received a BA from Dartmouth College and an MFA from California College of the Arts. She has presented recent projects at Northern Arizona University Art Museum (Flagstaff, AZ), Esqueleto Gallery (Oakland, CA), c3:initiative (Portland, OR), Riffe Gallery (Columbus, OH), Wave Pool Gallery (Cincinnati, OH), and Pie Projects (Santa Fe, NM). Fletcher was a 2018 Artist in Residence at Headlands Center for the Arts (Sausalito, CA) and was awarded an Individual Excellence Award by the Ohio Arts Council in 2017. Prior artist residencies and awards include Anderson Ranch Arts Center, Sedona Summer Arts Colony, and the Murphy and Cadogan Award. Fletcher is a faculty member at the University of New Mexico.

Editor's Note: Below is an edited conversation between *On Transfer* guest editor Susannah Magers and contributor Welly Fletcher from July 2020.

WF: I totally appreciate your questions ahead of our call today. It's an interesting time to have this conversation in terms of reflecting on work I made before shelter-in-place, what I've been making, and then how much has changed in the last four or five months. In terms of my perspective and even thinking about what's gonna happen with art, it was useful to think and talk about.

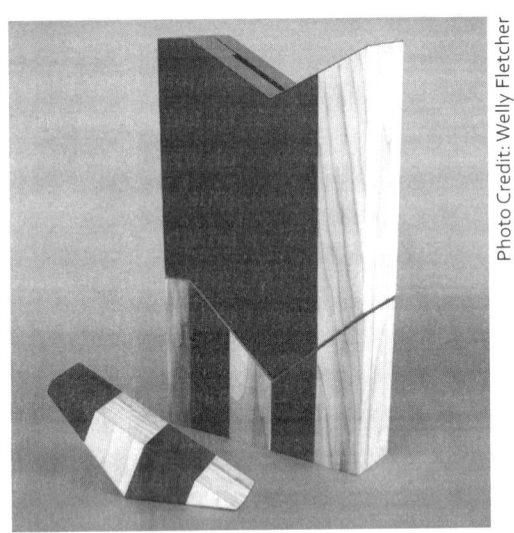

Welly Fletcher. *Totem for Diagonal Resistance - Contraposto Lipstick Lez Manylith*, 2018. Poplar, milk paint, leather, rayon flocking, wax; 17" X 12" X 2.75".

SM: Good! I've mentioned in prior conversations how hard it is for me to focus in general right now. I haven't looked at art in a museum or gone to a show in so long, since before quarantine. I think the last exhibition I spent time with was *Queer California* [at the Oakland Museum of California in 2019, which featured work by Welly's partner and fellow artist Amanda Curreri]. It was a while ago that I was physically in the space of an exhibition, which is of course not the only place to experience art, but I'm realizing that I feel so distant from that kind of experience. So, it was nice to read your review of the 2019 exhibition *Creatures* at Contemporary Art Center Cincinnati and then look at your website and experience the photos of your series *Shields for Queer Kin*. It was almost like living vicariously through the people in the photos and to be reminded of the scale and human proximity to these works and one way they are meant to be experienced. Seeing posts on social media right now where people can go see shows leaves me thinking about what it feels like to experience art in a socially distanced way: to be let in to view it by yourself, behind a mask.

WF: It's a completely different experience, not being in a room with work, and especially for me. It's like the root of everything for me is a body in a room and a space with other material bodies — the confrontation of that. It's been challenging and confusing to come up against the pandemic, but also the pandemic is happening in the context of all of these protests and this huge cultural revolution. So, there are also those questions, but we're grappling with them in private. The artwork in my studio, that's, like, not going anywhere very soon.

Photo Credit: Tom Alexander

Welly Fletcher in collaboration with Amanda Curreri.
Shield for Queer Kin: Protection, 2018.
Sashiko embroidery, soot-dyed cotton over steel, cedar; 5.5' x 4' x 4' 2".

SM: That's a nice thread to unravel. How does knowing that the work won't necessarily be experienced in the way that you thought or had initially intended? That's always a question, pandemic or not. What are your intentions for the experience of the piece and how does it confront what actually happens? Does that change the way you're making work — giving yourself permission to make work that is not for consumption right now?

WF: I think I'm split on that. My studio practice now is shaped by this big move from Cincinnati to New Mexico as well as coming off of a year of being in a full-time job that is — as you said when you sent me questions ahead of this conversation — in the service of the arts, but not art-making. It's been a big palate cleanser, and at the same time, there's some relief in showing up to the studio with a reevaluation of my practice, themes, and whiteness — the work I feel has to happen right now, for everyone, whatever relationship you have with whiteness, digging deeper.

And so, bringing that energy into my studio, I guess there's a relief in having space to do that work, to be in the context of the work I've made, and then just be here and let it mix. I feel I'm more and more trying to practice that way: to rigorously work hard at transforming my mind, learning new things, shifting perspectives, but I don't boss myself around. I trust that the rational, intentional, emotional, and social work will feed the other levels of consciousness that I connect to in my art practice.

There's a tension between the relief that I have this space to do that and this weird feeling and fear of naval gazing if I don't have a public exhibition where there is visual communication with someone that's not me. Do you know what I mean? I'm never relieved or comfortable or at ease right now. But to be able to have that tension in private makes me feel like I can pay more attention to and learn from it instead of blocking it out and just getting something done for a show. That quite honestly seems like the absolute least important thing right now.

It feels like about every five years I go through a total overhaul and ask myself: what have I been doing? What are all the problems with what's here? Where does it fall short? How do I take the next step?

SM: So, you're in an educational position now as assistant professor in the sculpture area at the University of New Mexico. What are you adamant about transferring, and not transferring, to your students? Are there strategies in the various aspects of the educational process that you are upending and challenging (for example, syllabus, guest speakers, evaluations, etc.) that you're calling on to mirror the questions of representation in how and why we make art?

Welly Fletcher. *Totem for Diagonal Resistance*, 2018. Basswood and purpleheart; 84" x 24" x 12".

WF: I get excited about that question. The themes that I want to carry over and expand on are the examples of transformation that feel so few. And I feel like I spend so much of my time in the art context in a critical mode. I've been trying to watch that, though I know that it comes from a place of questioning, "Hmm, that doesn't quite do it" or, "It could do more." I've been reading Octavia

Butler and N.K. Jemison, who both ask: what can the future look like? And I feel like that's where artists can dream. My artwork isn't a continual critical reflection of the world. It has counter-punches in it, for sure. The *Many-liths* and *Shields for Queer Kin* are all diagonal pieces, leaning and off-center and supported by many things in order to counter a heteronormative monolith — this is a queer many-lith, you know, like, it has its own strength and isn't just one singular thing. It's not about something else; it's about itself. It's responsive and composed of many bodies.

Photo Credit: S. Long

Welly Fletcher. *Shield for Queer Kin*, 2017. Hydrocal and Portland cement, heat formed and patinated steel, wool, felt; 72" x 48" x 48".

I'm here teaching and think, what can it look like when art-making isn't driven by fear and anxiety about basically not having enough money? That feels like so much of what happens — art institutions and educational institutions, and decisions come down to that. I won't be interested in teaching if money becomes the priority, the transfer. Part of me wonders as these institutions potentially crumble at their bases, definitely weakened, there's potential to build something totally different.

    I was listening to a Fred Moten talk the other day — as well as reading bell hooks' *Teaching to Transgress* — and I'm learning from these humans that are playing that line of transgressing what the institution does, but actually staying in it. It's not burn it all down and start fresh, but it is totally undermining, refusing, reforming. I feel like those are some of the teachers along with science fiction, humor teachers (Dynasty Handbag), who are not trying to sit down and figure it out and fix it in a way that uses building blocks that already exist. I think we just need to invent some totally other building blocks. I want to be a part of that, so I have to unravel the ways I'm caught up in the world as it is that I'm not conscious of. I still have work to do on that because everything in the world encourages me to stay exactly where I am. As a teacher, in my classroom, instead of standing up to give a lecture, I work to pass the mic to facilitate a way for artists who have way more important things to say right now. I have to learn from them to shift power.

    SM: I have a very complicated relationship with my time in grad school and the legacies from that. When people ask me now about going to grad school, I pause and usually reply with something about making them pay you, and whatever you do, DO NOT take out a bunch of loans to do it.

    WF: The University of New Mexico, which is where I am, is so educational for me. I think my image presentations are broad and ranging. And then I come here and I'm like, "Oh no — what I'm offering is *still* so biased and narrow in ways I hadn't yet considered." I've got artists from all over the globe, different races and cultures, but it's still relational to a canon that needs a prerequisite in order to decipher. One of my guideposts, for example, if I'm teaching an intro to sculpture class, is that students leave the class with a visual language that preps them to not be excluded when they go to a contemporary gallery because it can feel alienating. I definitely was alienated by contemporary art before graduate school. I didn't understand a lot of the theory. I hadn't been exposed to it.

SM: So much of what we learn in grad school wasn't made for us, or with us in mind.

WF: True. And then iterating that now, and realizing whoa, this is a limited shred of what art is and can be. Sure, this can help you understand what the Whitney Biennial is talking about or Documenta, but it certainly isn't like the guidepost to then make your decisions about what comes next or could come next. So, then, is it even useful talking about it?

Photo Credit: Tom Alexander

Welly Fletcher in collaboration with Lukaza Branfman-Verissimo. *Shield for Queer Kin: What Does Support Look Like?*, 2018. Plywood, paint, patinated steel, laser cut industrial felt, purpleheart, cedar, basswood; 76" x 66" x 52".

SM: I want to return to this idea of being in service to art. We have both been in many stages of transition since our last studio visit at the Headlands Center for the Arts [in Sausalito, California]. We've been moving from state to state, changing jobs, and experiencing all of that against the backdrop of a socio-cultural paradigm shift (for the better, of course!), and the associated turbulence that always comes with standing up to power and refusing to be under the thumb of a white supremacist, patriarchal system. You spent the past year managing a production studio. As I understand it, this was similar to what I'm doing (and have been doing) around my writing practice. I write full-time, as a job, but not in service of the arts most of the time. Writing is a muscle and skill and exercise for me that's being deployed for different applications. And it can be tricky to move in and out of these worlds, to context switch. What came up for you during the year you took off from being the studio full time and how has this influenced your work? What surfaced for you in relationship to your conceptual and theoretical methodology and frameworks? You are now back in a space of focusing on your work and on your position as an educator. What was that journey like?

Welly Fletcher in collaboration with Hannah Ireland. *Shield for Queer Kin: Time Given Back to the Body*, 2018. Clay, looped video on digital screen, brass, wood, stone, felt; 38" x 36" x 14".

WF: That's a lot of transfer! During my residency at the Headlands, I was told that my job that I had argued for a certain salary was going to be cut by 20% for the same amount of work.

That forced a transition: to either suck it up and do it or rally all the energy and work it takes to make a change. The change I made was to get this technician job that paid well at the University of Cincinnati to manage this brand-new makerspace. I went in, and for the first time, was setting up welders and going to "waterjet camp" in Seattle. I wasn't trained as a sculptor, and I would say in the first ten years of my art practice, every project I did I was trying to learn something else about how to make stuff that I was curious about. I'd come up with this project, and I'd figure out how to use the CNC router or how to mill metal. So this job was this cool combination of getting paid to know how to do a bunch of stuff, but then also getting an opportunity to learn a ton of new skills and get more fluent with my current ones. Fluent in a way that doesn't have to do with me coming up with art projects but just has to do with doing it all the time. I learned so much, but it was really physically exhausting. It made me realize, with all the jobs I've had, that it's always been about, like, how do I find the energy to balance that with the studio practice? If I'm on the computer all day, even though that sucks, then I have energy to go make stuff. But if I'm painting houses all day, which I did for a couple of years, or in the makerspace being an extrovert, all I want to do afterwards is sit down. Finding that balance and the skill building has been really significant. Coming out of it, I knew my body couldn't sustain that work that many hours a day. I'm such an introvert that having eight to nine hours of constant interaction is just not good for me. I'm more of a sprinter when it comes to extroversion, not a cross country runner. This teaching job has helped me understand I need to balance my energy, and I appreciate the time that I have that I'm not bound to be somewhere. I can't take everything so seriously. I do that in my studio and if I'm doing that at work, it's just a gnarly combo. I'm constantly trying to loosen up in that way.

I'm also just wondering if maybe, maybe there's a way that I'm going to, like, um, figure out how to step off the stage more, but still be an ally of the art. Let the sculptures do the speaking in their own weird language. Not feel I need to supplement them or translate with my voice, performance, words. The cool thing about teaching is that I can forge new strategies, like have everyone teach something about monuments, which is what I'm doing this fall. This last semester, I consciously for the first time with an advanced sculpture class, tried as much as I could to not take up space. Sure, I'm the teacher and coordinator of the class, but I don't have to occupy more space than anyone else. I'm working at undoing those things and then making alternate forms where we're sharing skills and learning from one another, you know?

SM: You mentioned you're working smaller in terms of scale. Tell me more about that.

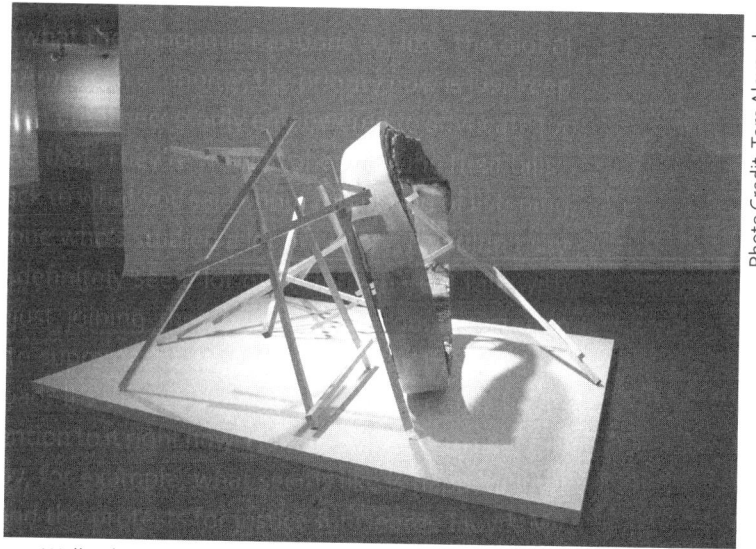

Welly Fletcher in collaboration with Terry Berlier. *Shield for Queer Kin: Nonorientable Lavender Menace*. Basswood, poplar, rubber, packing blanket, industrial felt, scotchbrite, copper, Magic-smooth, turmeric; 84" x 72" x 47".

WF: I'm making really tiny artworks right now — powerful little potent action figure-type things. I came from making these last big series, *Shields for Queer Kin* (or *S4QK*) and *Manyliths*. Being literally not straight, no right angles, the orientation of those structures feels like the most obvious abstract move. And the collaborative *S4QK* pieces came out of a real need for deep connection, being in a new city when we moved to Cincinnati. Collaboration is a way that I can find a new language. If I have a certain lexicon, I don't want to be stuck in it. And so, these collaborations were like ways of having long-term conversations about what's happening in the world but challenging ourselves to generate a form at the end of it, you know? Four large-scale sculptures came out of that with Terry Berlier, Hannah Ireland, Amanda Curreri, and Lukaza Branfman-Verissimo.

Then I have these smaller series I'm just beginning, but are really making me think a lot, with those teachers/writers I mentioned earlier, in mind and heart. I brought all my Star Wars action figures out. I'm thinking about inter-alien animals, human-exceptionalism, superheroes as everyday people and planet-materials. I have these small miniature figures that I've made in all of these different materials that fit together. I'm thinking about bodies that aren't singular like my body: it is made up of many things — my community, my society, my job, all the people I engage with — an anti-monolith; they kind of all fit together. And then I've been lining them up, seeing how they interact. I've made some small bronze animals, too, that sit with my smaller sculptures and give them this feeling of immensity, but in their tiny totemic scale, which is only, like, five inches. I'm sitting with them. I'm not sure yet what comes next. The next chapter has not been written of what these are. They aren't quite ready to go out in the world.

SM: I mentioned scale because looking at *Shields for Queer Kin*, I'm thinking about, who they are for? What space do they literally take up? What do they represent? And who are they protecting?

WF: It's more about asking, who are the shields as presences themselves? I took the long way around to sculpture where I started by making things that you inhabit, framing the body of the participant to come inside and make contact with. In *Shields for Queer*

Kin, the material bodies and the combination of wool, felt, steel, stone, and wood — the material bodies are the *bodies*. It's about their presence, their strength and vulnerability in tandem, and how they're off-balanced and supported. There are many components supporting other components. The bodies that need protection are fiercely strong. I'm not totally vulnerable, but it's sort of like in Judith Butler's *Violence, Mourning, Politics*: it's in our shared vulnerability that we can find empathy and communion with one another. It's a source of great power and strength. There is something powerful to be confronted with that scale of that much material.

Installation view of *DIAGONAL RESISTANCE* // a 2018 exhibition of the work of Welly Fletcher, and featuring work in collaboration with Terry Berlier, Lukaza Branfman-Verissimo, Amanda Curreri, and Hannah Ireland. Northern Arizona University Art Museum, Flagstaff, AZ.

SM: As we see the dismantling and uprooting of oppressive institutions and hierarchies in the policing and cultural commemorative systems (quite literally toppling statues and sculptures and objects that have for so long stood in as static representations of power), what conversations are you most interested in starting about representation and collaboration as a practice?

WF: This is an exceptional time in cultural history, with the Black Lives Matter movement leading a revolution in broader cultural empathy and action regarding the long-term inequities and racism faced by BIPOC citizens. As part of this movement, I've been particularly struck by and engaged with the debates newly invigorated around public monuments and their role and responsibilities. Many of these objects have been targeted as physical markers upholding racist values and histories, and community calls to discuss their removal have evolved into swift actions of removal and re-facing.

This fall, I have been participating in the Race, History and Healing Project launched by the City of Albuquerque in response to community concerns about the Oñate statue, which is part of *La Jornada* public art installation on the grounds of the Albuquerque Museum — a commemoration of 400 years since the colonization of New Mexico by the Spanish. The process centered a series of community Dialogue Sessions, where interested community members discussed the statue and surrounding issues through a series of small group, professionally facilitated sessions with each other. The goal was to gather a community-based set of recommendations to the city for the future of the artworks. Basically, what do we, as a community, need from our public artwork? And what needs to go ...?

This process was so intense, so painful. We all spent over eight hours on Zoom over the course of a couple months, in highly facilitated sessions, talking about core values, our cultural inheritances, what we need from public art. The pain caused by these monolithic, heroic public artworks all over the country that are — as you said — static, enduring, durable representations of power is so palpable, so unfair, so seemingly unending.

So, I've been doing a deep dive on the role and strategies of public artwork, thinking through what it's made out of, how long it lasts, which histories it upholds and validates, and how the materials, representations, form, height/pedestals, and space is taken up to re-enforce power structures. So, that leads me clearly to wonder, as a sculptor, as artists, how do we use these same tools (materials, representations, form, pedestals, space) to *un-do*, to *re-monument*, to *dismantle*. An Acoma Pueblo elder in one of my small groups during the RHHP put it succinctly, "we need art that honors all."

So, my question, in my studio, with my students, as I keep reading and attending and witnessing, is how do we do that? What does it look like? I can imagine what that *feels* like, but how do we start really exploring how those forms, or spaces, or engagements manifest in physical form? Maintaining *meaning* and *impact*, harnessing the power abstraction can provide, not letting it fade forms into blurry big nothings.

The artwork made in contra-distinction to the *La Jornada* sculpture for the Cuarto Centenario Project here in Albuquerque was a powerful artwork by Nora Naranjo Morse. *Numbe Whageh* (2005) is a real starting point for me to imagine how we might do that. It's made of the land (the longest-lasting material!), in the land, for the land, in the visual language (material, form, representations, etc) of the Pueblo peoples of Northern New Mexico. I think it might work on every level. *Numbe Whageh* and the re-faced Robert E. Lee statue in Virginia are my current guideposts for moving forward.

DIVING AT THE LIP OF THE WATER

Karen Poppy

I am the wall at the lip of the water
I am the rock that refused to be battered
I am the dyke in the matter, the other
I am the wall with the womanly swagger
I am the dragon, the dangerous dagger
I am the bulldyke, the bulldagger

From "She Who," by Judy Grahn, at the beginning of Chapter Six of her book, *Another Mother Tongue*, about the linguistic history of the word bulldyke/bulldike.

The common duiker [a small antelope, name pronounced dyker] uses a pair of glands under its eyes for scent marking with a tarry secretion. Duikers run with a distinctive darting and diving style when they flee danger. This gives rise to its common name which is the Africaans for "diver."

From the website of Fascinating Africa.

Between trees, within edges
Of forests, woodlands.
Among open clearings.
With scent markings below eyes,
We label another our own.

This is how we bull duikers do it.
We males secrete a substance,
Deftly labeling, marking with
Our tarry, leaf-scented names,
Our territories, calves, mates.

When we run, we dive at the lip
Of the water, be it a field, a deep
Forest, a body. We do this from love
Or fear—which you understand,
For you and I mark in the same way.

—

Humans cover with other scents,
Afraid of labels or diving into them.
Each marking, energy, power.
Labels we give ourselves,
Labels we use to mark another.

Some names change in meaning,
Mutate over time, original markers
Lost. Some we mistake in origin:
Bull duiker, a male antelope.
Never the origin of bulldyke.

We cull meaning from sound,
Just as our eyes tell us what
We see. We feel. An energy,
A power. You misread her,
By mistake or by design.

—

We can only guess at origin
Of bulldyke and bulldagger.
Roman times. Harlem Renaissance
Novels. Women singing the Blues.
Dig within erasure and resistance.

I like the Blues best, the song
Written and sung by Bessie
Jackson (pseudonym of Lucille
Bogan)—explicit and raw,
Prophetic dirty Blues, peel

Back the layers, and here
It is, lay of the land. Women
Can be whatever they choose:
Comin' a time, B.D. women
Ain't gonna need no men.

—

"Bulldike is the kind of word
Most women hope to avoid
All their lives, for few things
Are more horrifying to be called,"
But these women hold the dagger.

Surrounded by hostile bulls.
Sometimes surrounded by
Women afraid of difference.
Sometimes by people who
Insist that she must be a man.

We can reclaim the name
"Used on a woman like a whip."
We can reclaim our own swagger.
Our own swagger can be womanly.
Our swagger can mark our love.

—

So says my lover, who loves me
Body and soul. There must be
Space for everyone. For women
Who swagger. For all women.
Don't say she isn't lesbian because

She loves me. There must be space
For her. For me: queer, never quite
Within borders, between, on edges,
In the open. I want to make that clear.
Embrace and don't isolate us.

Surround us with love, define us,
Mark us by our love for each other.
I love a woman, but my gender bleeds
Beyond labels and markings, no matter
What I'm called, and what you call me.

—

No matter what I call myself, I am marked.
I bleed monthly. I've been attacked with
Thrown stones, called a dyke. I swagger
Womanly, and I love a woman, but
I am not one. I swagger, and I shift.

—

We have to love each other.
Those on either side of gender
Binary. Those who transform,
Transgress—and those who
Stay hidden in heavy cover.

Also those like me,
Who don't fit evenly,
Who shift and move
Without gender, and
Within sexuality.

Some things, especially hate,
Can mark you. They have
Marked me. Call me what
You will. I love you,
As I do, unconditionally.

—

I will love my lover,
Knowing her beauty
Shakes the earth, comes
From another place, full
Of energy, power.

The sleek duiker dives
In escaping run, zig zags
Like my lover's tongue—
But my lover is not afraid.
My body a safe field, a sheltering forest.

She cleanses me, recitations
Of sacred ash, this beautiful
Burning, a pooled release.
When I cry, I am hers, and
I am her. She holds me.

—

There lived a warrior queen named
Boudica. Bulldike, or bulldiker.
In a last stand, with warrior daughters,
Boudica burned Londinium,
Now modern London, to the ground.

She led a vast uprising when Romans
Invaded to destroy her people.
What happens if we erase her name?
What happens to our own markings
Of energy, power? Let her be named.

Let us dive at the lip of the water,
Into love, and fearless. Let us
Mark each other with freedom,
Like bold Boudica at the helm
Of the chariot, horses charging—

No one holding the reins.

Editor's note: "Diving at the Lip of the Water" is previously published in Karen Poppy's poetry chapbook *OUR OWN BEAUTIFUL BRUTALITY* (Finishing Line Press) and as a feature poem online in *Cultural Daily*.

Karen Poppy has work published in numerous literary journals, magazines, and anthologies. Her chapbooks *CRACK OPEN/EMERGENCY* (2020) *and OUR OWN BEAUTIFUL BRUTALITY* (2021) are both published by Finishing Line Press. Her chapbook, *EVERY POSSIBLE THING*, is published by Homestead Lighthouse Press (2020). An attorney licensed in California and Texas, Karen Poppy lives in the San Francisco Bay Area.

ON NICHE LESBIAN CONTENT, INTERNET COMMUNITIES, AND QUEER ADVICE
A *conversation with* Maddy Court

Maddy Court is a writer and zinemaker from Wisconsin. Her first book, *The Ex-Girlfriend of My Ex-Girlfriend Is My Girlfriend*, was published by Chronicle Books in May 2021. She also writes a weekly newsletter about TV and queerness called *T.V. Dinner*. Find her at maddycourt.substack.com

SM: First things first — how did you get your meme account started on Instagram [@xenaworrierprincess, which has over 67,000 followers at the time of writing this], and how did you decide to branch out into self-publishing?

MC: I started making memes in 2017. At that time, I was pre-Saturn Return and treading water in women's studies grad school. The idea for @xenaworrierprincess just sort of came to me at the Lesbian Herstory Archives. I was staying in Brooklyn and doing research there over winter break. It was the week of Christmas, and I was the only person in the building — just me and all this lesbian culture and history. The first meme I made was about a certain kind of butch you find on Tinder. Instagram was a lot simpler back then. There were no stories or long videos. I like social media, but I hate feeling sucked in or like I can't put my phone down.

I made the first *Ex-Girlfriend* zine a year later because I was scary-broke and needed money. UW-Madison, where I went to grad school, charges graduate students a "segregated fee" that's over $600 per semester. I could barely buy groceries on my stipend, and I was out of savings, so I was furiously brainstorming a way to capitalize off all the work I'd poured into @xenaworrierprincess. I sensed there was a demand for queer relationship advice because my followers would frequently send me questions like, "am I gay?" or, "how do I get over my ex-girlfriend?" *The Ex-Girlfriend of My*

Ex-Girlfriend Is My Girlfriend was just a more formalized version of writing that I was already doing. I made a lot of zines as a teenager, so zinemaking is work that feels comforting and familiar to me. I know how to fold and staple.

Maddy Court's first (and now sold out) zine.

I remember, early in the project, an order came in from Japan, and I realized that the zine was much bigger than me. I'm really grateful to everyone who evangelized *Ex-Girlfriend*. I never expected the zine to travel so far, or that I'd get to expand the concept into an honest-to-goodness book.

SM: As I read Volume 1, I was struck by the part of the intro about not being a gatekeeper of queer identity — that, while you give advice, this work is ultimately about your life and your experiences (thank you), and it should be taken as such. One of the aspects of @xenaworrierprincess I most enjoy is how unapologetically geared towards a specific brand of dyke culture it is, yet inclusive of the queer spectrum. How has your content and advice framing or methodology shifted since you began the meme [and then the zine] project? What has the feedback been?

MC: It's interesting to describe the memes as inclusive because I use the word "lesbian" or "dyke" in every single one. At the same time, I'm never trying to define or delineate what a lesbian is or who can enjoy the meme. A lot of people with lesbian parents follow me, so do a lot of bisexual and straight women. I love that they're in the audience. I felt territorial of lesbian identity when I was younger, but I'm old now, and I just don't have the energy.

Instagram Meme by Maddy Court.

When I write advice, it's just my own Sagittarian common sense. I try to choose questions that I feel like I can answer in a way that will be helpful and illuminating. I'm not qualified to answer a question about, say, dating and finding queer community as a wheelchair user. When I was putting the book together, I had a budget to compensate someone like Kalyn Rose Heffernan, an amazing disability activist, to share her lived experiences. The book is infinitely more interesting because Kalyn and the other guest writers contributed their wisdom and perspectives.

Occasionally someone gets mad about a meme or something I post, but with the zines I feel pretty insulated from criticism. I think people who seek out zines are more willing to roll with whatever. The book comes out this spring, and it will reach a wider audience, so I'm sure people will have words. I'm ready to get dragged on Goodreads.

As far as how my advice and memes have changed. I see things with a lot more nuance now that I'm older. I used to be more invested in "the discourse" online, but now I care more about my offline friends and community.

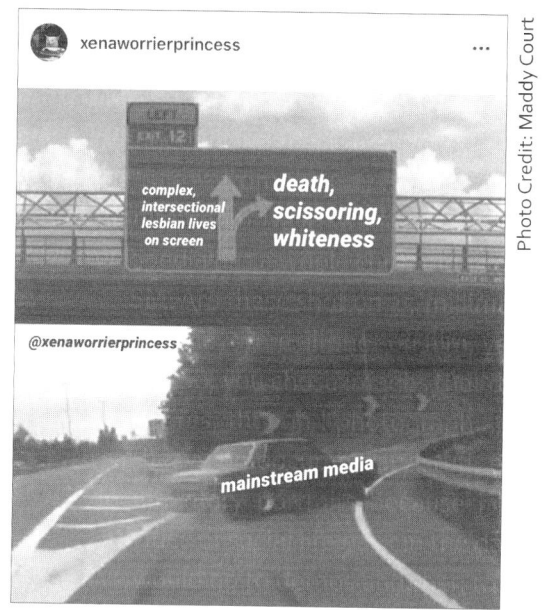

Photo Credit: Maddy Court

Instagram Meme with intersectional nuance by Maddy Court.

SM: One way I think about memes and their purpose is that they come from collective experiences which lead to generalizations (a word that gets a bad rap), but I think that there's a special power in "generalizations," especially for communities that don't see enough of themselves mirrored in popular culture. Or, when they are, it's super problematic, like *Basic Instinct*-level bad (I'm looking at you, *Tales of the City* reboot. Ok, it wasn't all bad...). What can generalizations do for the lesbian community as points of contact and opportunities to connect?

MC: I only watched the first episode of the new *The Tales of the City*, but it seemed like a project that was trying to do a million things at once. In my MFA program, I was lucky enough to study with Lynda Barry, and she taught me that when a story is about everything, it becomes about nothing.

All memes are generalizations, but I also think a good meme is hyper-specific. Sometimes the joke *is* the specificity. Sometimes the meme is that I'm trying to universalize something specific to me and not succeeding.

Instagram Meme commenting on online relationships by Maddy Court.

It's interesting to think about generalizations and lesbian memes because I think lesbian art and culture is often written off as niche or retrograde. In a lot of queer communities, there's a sense that lesbian stuff is only relevant to lesbians. One big example is how mainstream and queer media alike replace the word "lesbian" with "queer women," even in situations involving self-described lesbians. Gay men don't have this problem, unsurprisingly. It's frustrating because lesbian identity and experiences are so diverse, which is why I try not to use vagina imagery or pictures of thin white celebrities in my memes. I'd rather use a picture of a pan of spinach shrinking down or an everyday object like a shoe. I think specific things are funnier and more meaningful. So much queer Internet culture is like "you are valid," and it's like, what does "valid" even mean? What real-world experience does this speak to? The worst kind of meme is a vague statement followed by a reaction gif. I want to reclaim specificity for lesbians.

One of Maddy Court's favorite memes.

SM: On a related note: nuance and humor appear to be the main ingredients in a meme, and yet its "success" rides on how something potentially private and/or deeply personal lands with a super public audience (to this day, the meme about curated lesbian sex playlists and Bruce Springsteen songs cuts. Me. To. The. Core. "Brilliant Disguise" and "Tougher Than the Rest" — I mean, COME ON). It's pretty incredible that something like that can resonate so powerfully with so many people. But seriously: Why is it important to you to make, and for lesbian and queer communities to experience, deeply self-referential content like the kind you create? As a fellow cultural producer, there's so much (to a sometimes agonizing degree) that goes into creating something before it goes out into the world. When do you know when a meme has arrived or is "done"?

MC: I forgot about the Bruce meme! Someone actually compiled a lesbian sex playlist based on everyone's comments. I'm going to put it on right now.

I love that memes are something I can create in a reasonable amount of time. When you're an artist or a writer, it's so important to finish projects so you can build up momentum. I also write fiction, which is work that feels isolating and endless to me. I also write a weekly newsletter about dating and relationships called *Secret Girlfriend* [now *T.V. Dinner*]. It feels amazing to press send.

Meme by Maddy Court

All of my memes start with a phrase like "old sea dyke" or "fake top energy" that strikes me as funny. I often look to my journal for inspiration. Then I'll roll it around in my head and try to find the perfect image. The image and text have to work together, which is something I learned from Lynda Barry. If I'm not sure if a meme is funny or not, I'll send it to a few friends and ask them to be honest with me. Not everything I post lands. I'm still figuring it out.

Susannah Magers's favorite meme by Maddy Court.

SM: I loved your list of ways to get involved and practice self-care in one of the zines, in response to someone who wrote about coping with the constant barrage of Tr*mp's anti-everything policies (and the general horrors of living through the death throes of white supremacist capitalism right now). Customizing your list is important and essential to avoid succumbing to feeling numb/inaction (which is particularly easy to slide into right now with the constant scrolling through bad news on top of worse news). Also, I think lesbians are notoriously terrible at practicing what we preach when it comes to self-care [raises hand]. Wearing SPF wear (have you heard of Beall's?) and platform Teva's at the beach while looking for baby turtle tracks is my current main form of self-care. That, and donating to mutual aid funds and buying art from my queer friends and queer artists. How has your own list changed or expanded since you wrote this?

MC: I've yet to explore the world of SPF wear! I struggle a lot with putting sunscreen on my back, so an SPF shirt would be an elegant solution for me. Thank you for the hot tip.

That list feels slightly naïve, but what else do we have? I think everyone is confronting their own powerlessness and limitations right now. I don't think I realized how bad things would get back in 2017, which says a lot about my white privilege and naivety. Something I have been reminding myself and my friends is that you don't have to consume news 24/7. It's enough to get the information you need to be informed and act responsibly.

This summer, I spent a lot of time volunteering at a community garden that used to be a golf course. I've never gardened or grown vegetables before. It was so fulfilling to learn a new skill. Gardening takes a lot of patience, but there are new developments and growth every day. The garden where I volunteered is a space that includes all sorts of people, from children to people struggling with addiction. It was really lovely to spend time there.

What else? I smoke a lot of weed and do HIIT workouts. I draw and make watercolors. I'm writing a novel. I have two neurotic pitbulls who need constant love and exercise. One of my dogs, Homer, was severely abused by his previous owners. I adopted him because I also felt scared and hopeless. I've had him for eight weeks now, and I've been working on ways to reduce his fear and anxiety. He's making slow progress. It's so gratifying to see him coming out of his shell, sniffing around outside, and enjoying life for the first time.

SM: On finding queer community, "queer friendships are the magic to life." (p. 24 in Volume 3). I have this vivid memory of watching the last few seasons (I think? Maybe it was just one or two?) of *The L Word* live at a bar called The Mix in SF. It felt like a secret club to be there with so many other gay women, sharing space and spilling beer on each other, even if the show itself certainly had its flaws. What moments of dyke solidarity and queer kinship are you enjoying and finding IRL (pandemic notwithstanding) and online right now?

MC: Watching a TV show at a lesbian bar? That is my ideal night out. Sadly, I first experienced *The L Word* on DVD a few years after the series ended. I wasn't out yet, but being able to discuss the characters felt like the first entry point to talking to other lesbians. I remember thinking Shane was so hot and so butch. I did not understand Helena at all.

Honestly, I have not felt lesbian solidarity or queer kinship for a long time. I've been spending more one-on-one with the homosexuals and lesbians in my life. My friend and I are trying to visit every Wisconsin state park. Sometimes we are too tired to hike, so we just slam seltzers at the local dog park. I try to talk on the phone with friends as often as possible. I've gotten really close with some faraway dykes that I otherwise would've been too shy to approach. It feels like the pandemic has normalized reaching out or asking for a phone call, which I love because I live in a small town where there aren't many queer people.

SM: There was a rather strong reaction in Volume 3 in the bad dates section to karaoke (so many question marks, I felt attacked, ha — though the behavior described, hijacking a date to sing, is *not* cool) and I have to ask. Karaoke: yes or no? If yes: what's your go-to jam? (Mine oscillates between Patsy Cline's "Walkin' After Midnight" and "Alone" by Heart, which I've never seen as devastatingly perfectly performed, and not by me, ha, as I have then by a dyke at the White Horse in Oakland.)

MC: I love a karaoke atmosphere. I love to watch my friends sing, but I hate being on stage and performing. It's really uncomfortable for me! If I did have a song, it would be "Mr. Jones" by Counting Crows. It's a terrible song and not at all sexy or queer, but I think people would be into it.

SM: I had the absolute honor of serving Tracy Chapman when I worked at Tartine Bakery in San Francisco (circa 2013). Rumor had it she lived nearby (I never saw her at the Lexington Club, though she frequented there, too), and when she first came in during one of my shifts, I fell over myself to be the one to take her order — bread pudding, which is what she got every time. She was so peaceful, quiet, and tipped well. Who is a celesbian you have met or would like to meet?

MC: I love when celebrities tip well. I've never had any celesbian encounters at work. I saw Parker Posey on the street in New York, and while not technically a celesbian encounter, it was a blessing. In college, I was one of the editors of the feminist newspaper, so I got to interview every speaker and artist who visited campus. We interviewed Alison Bechdel, who actually read our paper ahead of time and referenced different articles and their authors. I remember feeling so astounded by how seriously she took the interview. We also interviewed Patti Smith and Judith Butler.

SM: What's something you have always wanted to write into an advice column about but never have? Or, if that's too personal, what's one of the best advice columns you read?

MC: I wish more people would send in questions about money. I'm really interested in personal finance and how money plays out in relationships. Everyone has a different relationship to money. It's so personal. There's a question in the book from someone who's supporting their girlfriend financially. They get a sense of control from being the provider, but they also resent their girlfriend for not helping more. Money is so emotional, but we're all supposed to pretend like it's no big deal.

I love Eshter Perel's podcasts. Most of the questions I receive are from young people who are new to dating or in comparatively casual relationships. I'm impressed by how Eshter tackles questions from couples whose lives are deeply intertwined with kids, property, or a cultural background that doesn't allow divorce. I also loved *Couples Therapy* on Showtime. Similar vibe.

SM: Ok, that about does it :) Did I leave anything out you would like to explore? I'm all ears. Thanks again for being available for this! And how do I get Nalu featured as a gay baby in *Secret Girlfriend*?! V. important.

MC: No, I don't have anything else to add! Let me know if you need anything else from me. Thank you so much for these thoughtful questions. Email me pics of Nalu anytime :-)

CLUSTER

Anna Olver

Anna Olver, *Cluster*. Watercolor and ink on paper.

Artist statement: *Cluster* is about finding beauty and love above ground. The fungi below the surface are difficult to get rid of but often go unseen. However, at the right time, they will show themselves above ground in the form of mushrooms. LGBT+ people thrive the same way. A mushroom, as well as LGBT+ people, can be vibrant and delicious and tenacious and unique because they came out of hiding with stronger roots.

Anna Olver graduated from Florida State University with her degree in Studio Art and Creative Writing. Her works have been featured in magazines, books, and galleries all across the USA. For more information on her and her work please visit her website: http://www.InkLinedArts.com.

ON BLACK BUTCH VISIBILITY
A *conversation with* Lenn Keller

Editor's Note: Lenn Keller died in 2020. *Sinister Wisdom* ran a remembrance of Keller by Rebecca Silverstein in *Sinister Wisdom* 120: *Asian Lesbians*. Keller's work has been featured in *Sinister Wisdom* multiple times.

Lenn Keller (September 29, 1951 – December 16, 2020) was a community archivist, historian, curator, DJ, filmmaker, photographer, public speaker, writer, and mother. She graduated from Mills College and was an independent scholar in multi-disciplinary, cross-cultural, and historical research. Lenn hailed from Chicago and lived in the SF Bay Area for over forty years. She documented, archived, and exhibited Bay Area activist and marginalized communities with an emphasis on lesbians of color and LGBTQ communities. Her first short film, *Ifé* (1993), won an audience award at the 1994 Women's International Film Festival in Madrid.

Keller's photographs appeared in *Aché: A Journal for Black Lesbians*, including a self-portrait she contributed for the cover of a 1991 issue. Five of her photographs — one is included in this issue — were included in a major 2019 group show, *Queer California: Untold Stories*, at the Oakland Museum of California. She founded the Bay Area Lesbian Archives in 2014, including her photographs and films and her collection of community flyers and posters from the 1970s.

LK: In the seventies, we didn't really get into gender very much because we were dealing with other things. In the eighties, after the BDSM community started becoming visible and helping people to become more articulate about their sexuality and to be more sex positive, people started to reclaim and started to be able to conceive of claiming butch and femme identities from within a feminist perspective. This was unheard of prior to that time. A lot of people *still* think that it's impossible, which I think is so ridiculous.

SM: That it's impossible to be a feminist and claim a butch or femme identity?

LK: An assumption I've observed is if you are claiming a femme or butch identity, is that you're not a feminist because — right? — because they think that the identities are inherently heterosexist.

SM: Tell me about your film project.

LK: The film is asserting femme and butch identities and dynamics can be feminist. People try to act like lesbians are passe. Lesbians are a dying breed. I've seen enough things come and go and people can believe certain things, very fervently. I remember how fervent we were — I was one of those people! I've been with femmes who said, yeah, we were so anti-butch/femme. That's just the way it was at that time. People misread and did not understand it. Even Audre Lorde didn't relate to either one of those identities, but she came of age at a time when it was forced upon you to choose. So, for every era or every age, there's a certain proper way to be a lesbian. In the fifties and sixties, it was either butch or femme. Whether that was appropriate for you or not, you better claim one, or you were a weirdo. You were pressured to adopt one or the other regardless of whether or you resonated with that or not. People assume that your identity determines who you're going to be with, and that's ridiculous too, because of course people are gonna hookup with all different kinds of gender identities. My observation is those people who identify as butch or femme are in the minority. And people who are into a butch-femme dynamic seem to be very much in the minority.

SM: Hmm, well, that's my dynamic. My wife presents as butch. But you're seeing that dynamic as not being prevalent or even politically incorrect at this point?

Photo Credit: Rebecca Silverstein

Lenn Keller passing the lesbian torch.

LK: It's been perceived as being politically incorrect. I don't think in actuality it ever was. I do believe that there are certain people who claim those identities who do act out heterosexist behaviors and attitudes — that's for sure. There's certain films like *The Aggressors* that perpetuate problematic butch stereotypes that veer into toxic masculinity. That's another reason why I think this film might be helpful to everybody regardless of their gender identity, to expand your mind a little bit, to just say there's some different ways we can think about some of these things that haven't been talked about because there hasn't really been space for it.

SM: How are you going to create that intentional space to explore these ideas in the film you're making?

LK: There's different sections that will deal with certain core issues around the butch-femme dynamic. One is how important it is for people that are in butch-femme relationships to understand what the public experience is like for their partner. Butches have to understand the layers of sexism, invisibility, and other shit femmes have to deal with. Femmes need to understand that butches, because of their presentation, are the more visibly, obviously gay people, and they have to deal with all this prejudice and discrimination. Char Ridenour made such an eloquent statement about these ideas when I interviewed her for the film. Those are the kinds of things that I think are important for people to understand. Butches deal with a lot of discrimination, with very real repercussions, just living your daily life surviving in this culture and society. You're more vulnerable to violence. It impacts everything: your livelihood, getting a place to live, mobility. I keep my happy ass in the Bay Area because I feel safer here than in many other places. There are places I wouldn't even consider traveling to because I don't feel safe. I don't feel like that's necessary for me to put myself in those kinds of situations. But that doesn't get talked about. There has been this legacy and the LGBTQ community around the acceptance of gender non-conforming people — specifically the LGB folks. The community has always been embarrassed by sissies and butches. I don't feel we've ever really come to terms with that, ever.

SM: How do you define sissy? I understand the term to designate a gay man — or is that gender non-specific?

LK: I define it as a feminine-presenting gay man. The community has always been embarrassed — do you have to be so obvious? I've heard tales from gay men, lesbians, and bisexual people what they've experienced from within the queer community around not being gender conforming. With HIV/AIDS in the eighties, all of a sudden, everybody tried to be all straight-acting. If you look at the personal ads from that time, all of a sudden, these ads specify "looking for a straight-looking man," "I'm straight-looking." Prior, there was lots of space for effeminate and flamboyant gay men. When HIV hit, certain folks within the queer community were marked. It was the same way for butches or for feminine gay men. We can't hide. You have to figure out strategies for surviving discrimination that you're experiencing in your own community, not just within the majority, heteronormative community. That's really deep because so many people went back into the closet.

SM: I want to frame this film you're working on about butch-femme dynamics as a form of transfer and the ways you're looking to reframe it. Where do you kind of situate yourself within that dialogue?

LK: I claim a feminist butch identity. I don't feel like I have a community right now, not a visible community. This film is dealing with this small little window from 1995 to 2005 when butch-femme reemerged very visibly. And there was an actual butch-femme community that was visible not only here in the Bay Area, but in other places as well, that didn't exist in the bars only. It was feminist. There were all kinds of events that were stated as this was like a butch-femme day. People came out and I mean, everybody was strutting and doing their thing. And it was, it was, it was like, wow.

SM: It sounds like you felt really seen.

LK: Yes, and validated. It was short-lived. And then it just kind of died down because the whole trans movement kind of superseded it. And so that was the end of that. I think the last interview I did for the film was maybe five years ago, but I might do just a few more because I want to get a few more younger people. A significant number of the butches I interviewed for the film have since transitioned.

SM: Let's talk about your work being included in the Oakland Museum exhibition, *Queer California*, looping back to this idea of transfer. Tell me about the process of being tapped to be in the show. What did that look like?

LK: I was invited to a convening, and there were maybe twenty of us, and we were asked to present our work. I made a PowerPoint, and I presented my photographs. There were historians, archivists, and artists. They asked me to contribute artifacts from BALA, and they asked me personally if I wanted to contribute photographs. They accepted five of my images. There weren't that many lesbians included in the show. I feel like lesbians are always an afterthought. I could just feel a palpable sense of these status tiers in the room, of who's important and who's not. It's a familiar feeling, unfortunately. Part of it is that I'm not an academic. There's a separate language that people who are in the academy speak, and I don't use that language. And even if I did know the language, I wouldn't use it because it's a hierarchical thing. It wasn't anything that freaked me out, but it didn't make me feel warm and fuzzy, that's for sure. I didn't feel embraced. It's just sort of like, okay, I'm here.

SM: What did you decide to show and what and why?

LK: This one is called *Black Lesbian Contingent*, and it was shot in the nineties.

Lenn Keller, Black lesbian contingent, SF Pride Parade, June 1991.

When I arrived in Berkeley in 1975, I moved into a lesbian household. There were all these dyke houses, as we called them, all over the place. They were usually named after the street that they were on. There was the Derby Street House, the Ellsworth Street

House, all these different houses. Gay liberation was focused on white gay men. In the Pride parade, the women were invisible, and, definitely, women of color were invisible. I went with signs against white male straight and gay supremacy.

SM: Wow! And how did that go?

LK: We were not alone. There were many women marching with those kinds of signs saying, let us in. So, they actually changed the name of the parade — what we now commonly know as Pride — from the Gay Freedom Day Parade to the Lesbian and Gay Freedom Day Parade. It just kept changing over the years. Wikipedia has a whole chronology of the shifting parade names.

SM: Are these shot on 35-millimeter film?

LK: They were all shot on film, yes.

SM: So, you chose images that depict celebration and protest?

LK: Yes, though I photograph a lot of different subjects. I am real heavy on documentary stuff, especially activism. I call them documentary portraits because I like to really hone in on the activities of social life back in the day, such as on demonstrations. We would go to demos and then to the club afterward. When I go to those demos, I really try to get into some specific moment that some person is having at the demo. I just like to kind of get it there and get some people's experience.

Editor's Note: Keller did not complete the film. Lenn's film and photography work are part of the Lenn Keller Collections of the Bay Area Lesbian Archives.

THE DEAD LETTER OFFICE
Elizabeth Train-Brown

I hope this finds you well
    god knows how I miss you
I'm writing to
    why am I writing
I'm writing
    I'm always writing about you

-

I didn't hold you then,
    didn't love you,
        couldn't.
What would they have said?
I'm not a dyke,
        alright?

(I just kiss girls in dark clubs,
ache in the night.)

-

I wrote these letters
and buried them here in this small,
four-walled space
where some people hang clothes
and some people hide.

They doused it in gasoline,
    lit it up,
danced in the flames,
    and I ran
from a pillar of smoke,

from a closet that
wailed like a child.

-

I cry in the night.
I am haunted by a little girl who has my eyes.

What do you write
to a child buried in the ashes
of a closet she burned in?

(I'm sorry)

I'm sorry
I couldn't lift you from the wreckage
of the hole we hid in,
dust down your pinafore,
take your hand and kiss your grubby cheeks.
I'm sorry I could never say

-

Do you know,
the Lady of my heart, who sang
baby, you were born this way,
twirls the stage,
laughs
when they ask,
men or women?

Agent Scully said
she would rather
honour a lost love
than hide.

You know,
the girl who ran with vampires
told them all,
I'm like so gay, dude.

And the girl who walked through walls
and played a white violin,
stood in front of a room of queer kids
to say,
I'm tired of lying by omission.

-

I'm writing to
    why am I writing
I'm writing
    I'm always writing about you
to tell you
that it's coming.
You just need to wait, my love,
to be strong.
I promise –
give it time
because,
in a few years,
they still won't love you

-

(but I will)

-

    Not known at this address, please return to sender

GLIMPSE

Elizabeth Train-Brown

I breathe out
and
she breathes in
pressed so close
hearts echo
staccato
through linen.

BRISK 'O

Elizabeth Train-Brown

lazing in the afternoon
on the grass.
sun-kissed and sun-touched.
Your eyes flitter,
like the birds,
dance across the sky
in sidelong swathes.
dart between the sycamores
and snag.
Our son,
that wild thing,
leaps and prances
across the grass,
sun-kissed and sun-loved.

Elizabeth Train-Brown is a multi-award-winning poet and novelist based in Lancaster. Twice-nominated Poet of the Year, Elizabeth has been published over 50 times in anthologies and journals across the world. She has appeared as a guest lecturer on LGBTQ+ issues for Lincolnshire's Annual NHS LGBTQ+ conference and has received national recognition for her journalist work with the LGBTQ+ community from LA Red Table Talks, Beyond Monogamy, and The National Tab. Her poetry collection, *SALMACIS*, an exploration of gender identity through pagan myth will be published by Renard Press in August. Find Elizabeth online at bethtrainbrown.journoportfolio.com and on all social media as page @BethTrainBrown.

ON MAINTAINING A SUSTAINABLE CREATIVE PRACTICE AND CARRYING LOOSE ENDS
A conversation with Kara Q. Smith

Kara Q. Smith is currently Manager of Programs and Organizational Advancement with Californians for the Arts. Prior, Kara was the executive director of Gallup MainStreet Arts & Cultural District in Gallup, NM. She has more than thirteen years of experience working for museums, galleries, and non-profit institutions. She has curated exhibitions, spoken at art fairs and symposiums, officiated workshops and lectures, and written for numerous publications. Kara also currently holds an adjunct faculty position in Sierra Nevada University's Interdisciplinary Arts MFA program.

SM: Thinking about this conversation today, I went back to where the idea to do this issue on the concept of transfer came from — an issue of *Sinister Wisdom*, *The Art Issue* Number 73, Summer 2008. The issue is mostly visual, with one photograph, painting, or drawing per page. What struck me is even the *Notes for a Magazine*, an intro from the current journal editor who was Fran Day at the time, is a picture of the edited manuscript of the issue laid out on a bed in Sebastopol, CA. I tapped back into that initial feeling of looking at this photograph of the manuscript of *The Art Issue*, laid out on the bed, and what it means to visualize the kind of work that we do as writers, editors, and curators — behind-the-scenes kind of work. That this would be Fran's choice to represent the work she does in this way is lovely.

I've been thinking a lot about what it means to stop and look at the trajectory you've been on and evaluate what's next. We've talked about this as a curatorial dilemma, but it's also a creative dilemma — knowing how to pursue the life we want, what happens when we can't, or when we're no longer willing to bend, twist, and literally move to accommodate it and make it happen.

Let's start with the notion of geography. You had written about defining a literal, spatial geography of where you live and the work you're doing. But also, conceptually, what does it mean to have moved your whole life to Gallup New Mexico for your work? Because I feel we're groomed to be hypermobile in order to do this work of curating; always teeing up other opportunities. Maybe that's not the case for you, but I'm curious where you're at with this concept.

KQS: Personal geography is complex. A place can push you out, or you can feel done, or terminated on your part or the place's part — a moment arises that feels right to leave it. And then it's like, how do you determine how and where you end up next from a spatial perspective? The way I felt like I needed to leave California was a very intuition-based thing, but it probably was relying on so many other factors, not only professional. Some people have this inherent calling or pull back to the places they're from — even if they moved to San Francisco or the Bay Area 20 years ago, they've always been planning to move back to wherever they came from at some point. But I think to switch it up, to go somewhere you're not from — that's what happened for me in thinking of the way a landscape can feel like it has potential in the way that it might hold a shift or a spiritual quality that's needed and that was different than California and also different than anywhere else. It's kind of a gamble; you're not a hundred percent sure. You're going on a feeling, a little bit of research and some factual qualities, such as there are artists in Albuquerque and Santa Fe that you know, there's a network of folks, but you're utilizing this bizarre internal temperature reader that comes out every once in a while. When you move to a new place, you follow that voice and land somewhere confidently, and then you try to do work in that place.

SM: What does it look like to begin in a new place?

KQS: And it's like, okay, cool. How do you do the same type of work? You go to the galleries, try to get coffee with people who work at museums, do studio visits with artists... And I think it's kind of like, the familiar place in the work that falls together, that helps me to feel like I'm doing the same thing, even though it's not called the same thing. By having this position in Gallup, part of an economic development nonprofit, all of a sudden, I find myself in the same familiar role now that I've settled in here for just a minute, given it a chance, and just gone for it. I recognize it when I speak with artists who come through town. These networks are built, and maybe that's exactly what this curatorial career is all about. I don't know if it's ever so much about the anchoring of places. It is about developing networks and connections.

I'm still untangling that. You need to be where you feel good, or you need to be where you think you need to be at the moment. Curating is a very unconventional career path and personal life trajectory.

SM: It is! I'm thinking back on when I moved to Minnesota and about what you said about making those connections when you first move to a place — how to do that genuine connecting work, that's on a personal and a professional level. I'm interested in what happens when you're kind of sitting outside of those systems, or if you don't necessarily have something to offer like an exhibition space or money or writing services or studio visit or portfolio review. As much as you said wherever you go, there you are — and there the work is — have you found that it's different in New Mexico or that this happens in a different way than it does here in the Bay area?

KQS: It definitely feels as if the whole rhythm and needs of the creative community are different because there's not as much of a concentration of artistic activity, especially from a commercial and museum-oriented standpoint. There's a different language around what it means to be a working artist and successful and productive. It's not that the terms or the end result isn't totally different, but that it's freeing to be outside of a concentrated urban area with multiple MA and MFA programs and competitive museums. What you get to transfer is a whole lot of skills that you don't need to worry so hard about applying everywhere in the same capacity as you did in the concentrated art centers. I don't need to worry too much anymore about going to an art opening. There's this weird lack of pressure, which creates challenges in the way you bring people together around contemporary art. That work is still there, but it feels very different. Artist statements, professional websites — in the Bay Area, these were part of an assumed tool kit you were supposed to have, so it's interesting to think about transferring what is truly relevant in this context. If you're working on projects, networking and doing relevant, meaningful things, then maybe you don't need those urban standards of what being an artist means.

A series of ricochets curated by Kara Q. Smith, installation view, Sierra Nevada University, January 2020. Featuring work by Valery Estabrook, nicholas b. jacobsen, Eric-Paul Riege.

What are we *actually* creating here? What are the materials and the things that are relevant to demarcate what it is to have our careers? Because maybe the meaning holds if the archive of what we produce is not there. There's this pressure — I feel like if I curated a show and you can't Google it, then does it exist? And I feel like it's similar for artists. Like, if you've worked on a project and you got paid to do it, but it's not on your website, what does that mean? We have created this realm of professionalism for creative careers, and I'm wondering now — how much of that codification is needed? I don't know. It's a funny place to be in.

SM: Say more about this idea of the relationship between your work and how it's archived because I would agree, specifically in the Bay Area because that's the arts community I know and can speak to the best, there's this validation framework, this burden of proof. You curate a show elsewhere; does it matter if it didn't get back to your network? If I did something in Minnesota or you did something in New Mexico, how does it live on in the world? Does it matter if it's not posted about on Instagram? Of course, I want to celebrate what people are doing. I'm happy for them, but it's this endless self-promotion. Of course, I'm going to post about this issue of *Sinister Wisdom* that I'm working on [laughs]. I'm part of it. We're all part of it, and I'm questioning this model of productivity or creative productivity saturation.

KQS: There are certain artists and types of people — I'm not one of them — for whom social media is a tool. I feel like an artist like Jillian Mayer builds their practice up through this idea of saturation in general via social media, but instead of stepping back to critique it, they actually *live* it. They make it, create it, and utilize social media as a mechanism of their practice or as a conceptual talking point. I became disillusioned with the role of social media in the art world, though, the role marketing and communications began to play in this over-promotional dynamic. Don't get me wrong — I'm an excellent marketing and communications person now because you have to be in the art world. That's how you develop relevance and validity, not just for yourself, but for the institution you're working for. Half of my job was promotions, documentation, putting together the right words for each platform, the wall label, and the public program. An entire staff engages in this immense promotional effort … and despite *all* of the work, you still get only ten people to an artist talk.

SM: We're all working away just to be able to be found on the Internet at some point in the future.

KQS: This is the question of the archive though. That artist's talk you promoted exists on YouTube and has digital threads all over the place, so in ten years, maybe someone discovers this talk happened at di Rosa in Napa with a ceramics artist that seems really great. I think about the show I curated in 2009 when I was in grad school, and nothing exists to commemorate it. The gallery shut down. There's absolutely nothing in the world except for you and the five artists that were in the show. Does that mean it wasn't a very good show? That it didn't have meaning? That I didn't do it right? What are those questions?

I carry a lot from that experience with me. It was a big learning curve and a great process for me. I don't know how the artists feel anymore. We were all young back then, but I keep that, and it's part of who I am and has helped scaffold who I've become. But it didn't get reviewed. There's not a picture of it, so it has this other quality, and all of the promotional work is the record, perhaps? This is where it gets a little weird for me with the self-promotional saturation. Every art museum, gallery, and institution has multiple people digitally curating their feeds. And then you have artists doing this digital curation for themselves as well, which begs the question: What are we doing in real life? It's like the experience that you get can be so tangible from just looking at your screen. I know that this sounds like an old lady thing to say, but I believe it's kind of an epidemic in the art world in particular because it's a visual culture. And all of a sudden, I felt oddly paralyzed. I actually didn't need to go to a lot of openings. I go because I care and want to support someone, but openings have become unfriendly. No one is asking you what you think of the work. The artists aren't even engaged. You know what I mean?

SM: Ugh, YES.

KQS: If we pull back the camera, why are we doing any of this? We care about art. We care about artists. We care about creativity, but why are we doing it this way? Because it doesn't feel good!

SM: No, it doesn't feel good. I don't go to openings much myself. If I want to look at the work, I'm going to go later when there's no one in the gallery and I can have space and time to take in the work. Or maybe I can make time to meet the artist, go look at it with them, and not feel like I have to navigate this awkward social structure of the opening. Because the quality in-person social interaction has been supplanted by the digital version of the experience, and there's such pressure to get something out of it. If you are a person who goes into this kind of situation expecting a real connection, someone asking you how you are and listening and not just being transactional, it's tough. There always seems to be a not-so-secret motivation: rubbing elbows with someone you want to work with, for example. These are things that are part of our work and what we have to do as cultural producers, and I'm not saying that's necessarily bad, but when the emphasis is on the transactional interaction, that's problematic for me. And that's the part that exhausts me. And it sounds like that's the part that exhausts you.

KQS: I'm not going to say I don't like going out, being seen, and having a glass of wine. I think that's great. I'm an urban kid. But when this is what you do all the time and you're paid to think very consciously about helping artists, contextualizing their work, bringing audiences in. But I also think there's a propensity to lose something in all of that. We've never found the right way to value, present, or finance it. Maybe you have to step outside of something every once in a while, you know? Maybe it's healthy to spend ten-ish years doing the same thing, the same kind of fight for space, equity, and pay for shows and artists you care about, but also space for yourself. And so maybe you just need a break to recalibrate.

SM: These are all good questions. Conversations like the one I'm having with you right now remind me of why I devoted so much of my life and time to art. How do we sustain these creative lives? How do we *not* transfer the problematic parts we learned or that we were groomed to transfer and still make it all work — financially and emotionally?

KQS: There are people who can spend a lot of time having opinions about things in the art world and casually running a gallery or intensely running a gallery. And they can care just as much, but they don't have the debt from the arts degree, and they don't have the same basic needs to fulfill with their work, like paying bills and healthcare. You want a job in the arts that sustains you *and* leverages your skills and training — but the art world is not built for that.

SM: Nope.

Community members paint an "Disarm Racism" mural, with artist Jerry Brown, on Coal Avenue in Downtown Gallup. June 18, 2020. Co-organized by Gallup MainStreet Arts & Cultural District.

KQS: The structure of having a fair salary, health insurance, and a semi-okay work environment is important for me to be productive, grow, and to do better work. The art world is often not the place where that kind of security is offered. It depends on where you're at with your life, your other circumstances, and how much resiliency you have. Thinking of transfer, I'm thinking about how I value myself. I have these skills and I should be getting paid to do the work I do when I offer to edit an artist's statement or look at their work, but it's hard to put your brain in that space. So, we have this service factor in the art world, especially with curator labor — we're expected to give and give, and we want to do it for the reasons we talked about earlier, but sometimes, I don't know that I was built for that.

SM: I feel similarly. I feel I was naive to the implicit social contract of being an arts laborer — that you'll give a lot and not be compensated at all, or well — and I was idealistic when I first began my arts career. I definitely think that's how I was perceived, too, by people I went to school with. I genuinely wanted to help people, and that was looked down upon. I just signed on the dotted line for loans. My curatorial program discouraged me from working, but I had to work. You're right; the art world is not set up for people like me or you. I prioritize my relationships with people above all, and it costs me a lot. It's literally cost me jobs. I've been fired because I just won't do something. I'm not going to work with assholes. I'm not going to be treated like shit. And I'm going to fucking tell you if you're being a jerk and you're treating people like shit. It can be a burden, but at least I know I did everything I could in spite of the system. They grind us down, make us feel like shit, and we're expected to get a PhD — for an incredibly competitive job that pays $35,000 a year.

KQS: Is this kind of being taken advantage of particularly unique to the art world? I've had the same experience. Speaking again of idealism and naivete, I went into my graduate arts program thinking I was going to get transferable skills, that I would have mentors and build something meaningful. I'm a consummate professional. I wanted to work, to be a part of something, and you don't get that in MA programs. And now you have this intense experience, and this degree, and it's forever. Every time you consider taking a job, it's like, okay, well, I did pay a lot of money to go to school for this. It shifts you ever so slightly, or at least hangs around. It's not a straightforward career navigation.

SM: Exactly, and it's because of that experience that I'm not going to transfer that brand of pedantic, holier-than-thou framework or recommend people go to graduate school. I look back, and I think, well, I did this thing. I committed and got the curatorial practice MA. It *did* matter. I worked *hard*. I did get things out of it. I became a stronger writer, for sure. But I think where the personal ethical and existential crisis came in for me was when I realized how much I would have to accept that goes contrary to my values and how much I would have to assimilate to be successful in that system. And I don't think that's just my pride and my ego. I'm committed to not perpetuating systems of abuse of power. Professors slept with students and even married them — and these professors are who I have to use as a reference when I leave this program, so it's a form of forced silencing. And I just can't do that. So, I realized I had to opt out. I knew the consequences of not condoning that behavior and not just turning away. I knew I was shutting myself out, and that it would cost me those connections and career opportunities. What do we have to sacrifice to not transfer or participate in these problematic arts non-profit models and still do the work?

KQS: Well, I somehow magically found a weird way to pivot by removing myself geographically from the Bay Area and somehow landing a position with many components that are new to me, but that center relationship-building and that underscore visual culture as an important element in our society and economic development in rural areas. So, it's possible to do the work outside of problematic systems. The place I'm in now is not set up like an art institution, which is good. But I think even if I had stayed in the Bay Area after multiple traumatic work experiences, I probably would have chosen to opt out myself. We have a huge leadership issue at influential institutions, from academic to museum organizations. It's a top-down issue, related and tied into boards, funders, and funding. But the minute we take all-male leadership or same-type-of-person leadership away and replace it with something else, there is potential. It's on the learning centers like CCA, SFAI, and SFMOMA to start critically thinking about what it should look like to work in the arts in a sustainable way: what healthy professionality looks like, what taking care of employees looks like, what treating employees like, what creating a pathway for someone looks like that's this. None of those things exist now in our institutional paradigms.

SM: I resonate with how you described moving to New Mexico for your current executive director role as a personal and professional pivot. What are some things you've carried with you that you are transferring that feel good and useful?

KQS: First and foremost: building relationships, learning and hearing other peoples' stories. Being a part of the fabric of a different place is especially valuable when you first show up somewhere else. It's a chance to start anew with and reframe social systems you are used to: taking public transportation, going to bars and restaurants, to openings at the local museum, being with friends who are like you. Everyone's curious about you; you're the new person. They want to know what it's like somewhere else, to bounce off ideas — what have you seen before? I carry a lot of threads with me; projects I did or didn't do that I still think about. Who knows when these loose ends might be fertilized? Maybe I'll be here for a couple years, and someone will call me from other places I've been and say, let's do this rad residency program together, or let's collaborate on something in two different states. I think I bring a lot of passionate optimism. It's not like I came here to assert myself and be the crazy liberal in town [laughs]. It's more important to me to hear how *other* people live their lives in a completely different area because it's not the Bay area. It's not where everyone has an ingrained vocabulary or a sense of 'do-gooder'-ness. I'm recalibrating what it means to be a part of a place.

SM: Anecdotally, where is a recent instance of you asserting your passionate optimism?

KQS: We are trying to think about increasing economic vitality and development. I'm working on a mural with an approach to make sure this community is represented: where it's going, where it's been. A mural is more complicated than just painting a wall. How can it be contemporary and engaging in this landscape? We are also talking about putting parklets in our rural downtown, and I am able to pull examples from San Francisco. I think I bring this, like, this lack of staidness, but this is also how I worked in the Bay Area, too. I don't know. It's something that I have inherently, but it's also, inherently, you integrate into a new area because you're fresh, the different person, voice, and perspective.

SM: What artists are you working with for the mural?

KQS: Her name is Marina Eskeets. So, she grew up here and went to school here in Gallup and then went on to school elsewhere and is now living in Albuquerque.

SM: What will the mural visualize?

KQS: We have a lot of murals in Gallup that depict the history, facts, and figures of our communities and neighborhoods. This mural is definitely a more contemporary, abstract, storytelling piece. It is her memories of sheep herding on the reservation growing up, with these larger-than-life graphics. There will be a storytelling event where we invite folks from the area to come and record their memories of sheep herding. And then you'll be able to, like, scan a little link and listen to them at the mural site.

SM: This conversation started with talking about failure, and I think we can safely say we've landed on failure being relative. Do we define failure by what we think we should have done based on the ideals that we're transferring to us?

Marina Eskeets mural in Downtown Gallup, *Óódááł | Everyone Moving Forward* (2019-2020).
Sponsored by Gallup MainStreet Arts & Cultural District.

KQS: And do we call it failure? The first time that I was "laid off" — which seemed like a veiled way of simply being "fired" due to an abusive boss — I thought my world was ruined. I thought, "I'll never have a job again." I fucking *failed*. But it's not true at all. It's fucked up psychology. I did an excellent job. I was totally qualified for the role. It took a very long time for me to work through and undo the trauma from that experience. You know what? No, I didn't mess up there. It was an unfortunate event. It leads to something else, and I don't have the rosiest worldview, but at the same time, I no longer consider being let go a failure. I contextualize those experiences within this bigger conversation about the art world often being problematic and our careers always being incredibly in flux.

CHERISHING/GUARDING LESBIANA: A MOVEMENT OF WORDS ON THE PAGE

Mev Miller

I remember my grandfather's studio. The room smelled of artist's oil paints and canvasses, and the walls were lined with books — floor-to-ceiling built-in bookcases swollen with all sizes, colors, and shapes of books. I aspired to create such a room for myself — not the paints, just the books and bookcases. And over the years, I have managed to do just that: every room features at least one bookcase, and my study is nearly wall-to-wall, including the closet with no door. And both the attic and basement contain bookshelves as well as many boxes of items that don't have space on the overstuffed shelves. I'm not maniacal enough to pull them out and stack them on floors, under the bed, or on the staircases (sometimes seen in pictures of the homes of great minds). I spare my partner that level of "clutter."

But I have been extremely selective about how my library developed over the years. I started quite young (age six) when I could begin selecting, collecting, and buying my own books. I realized too late in my career development that I should have become a librarian. And over the sixty-plus years as a book hoarder, my focus has turned over several times. Gone are many of the college-required books, followed by the theology books, and then the highly academic books I acquired as a book reviewer, the professional educator volumes, and finally the generally popular bestsellers.

Over the years, two categories of books have stayed with me to line all those bookcases and live in the many boxes; namely, an extensive library of lesbian, feminist, and women's studies books — all genres, including fiction, mystery, essays, nonfiction on many subjects, memoirs, biographies, and autobiographies — well, just about everything. In fact, easily 95% of my remaining library contains volumes written by, for, or about lesbians or women. My obsession blossomed not only by my personal interests but also through my twenty-five-plus years as a professional in the feminist/independent press book industry. Most items are from the 1970s - 1990s, but I have some newer books as well. I now fancy myself as a pseudo-librarian, book collector, archivist, and holder/guardian of hundreds of published volumes of lesbian words and ideas. And here is the dilemma: as each year passes more quickly, and I advance into my later sixties, I ponder and worry about how to care for these treasures going forward.

My collection of lesbian published words and art (and even music and spoken word recordings) began in the late seventies. I kept everything I acquired, mostly because I loved the feeling of all those lesbian creativities surrounding and living with me in my dwelling spaces. They became essential guideposts for my own developing radicalism. I felt that what I was collecting could very well be essential to my existence/identity as a lesbian, both then and into the future. As I became more directly involved in the evolution of the women's bookstore/publishing movement, I began to realize the herstorical importance of what I was holding. When I first heard about the Lesbian Herstory Archives sometime in the early eighties, I considered creating my own local archive. From my own political activism, I knew two things: "it's harder to hit a moving target" AND "decentralization makes a movement stronger." So, I have decided <u>not</u> to send my treasures to any of the already established archives (New York City, Chicago, Los Angeles, San Francisco). I suspect they already have what I have anyway, so better to create another outpost in a different geographical location. University libraries I know also have archival collections, but these are generally available for research purposes and not easily (if at all) accessible to a casual reader interested in searching through such publications for solace or insight and not affiliated with academia. I'm afraid a regular public library would, over time, one-by-one, rid the collection if it didn't circulate enough. And there is no stable LGBTQ center in our area.

I worry about keeping these many volumes with me in my home because I know that once my partner and I pass away, our family members will have no idea what all this "stuff" is. I can hear it now: "Damn her and all her books" as they lug them to whatever destination. Sure, in our wills we could state they should be sent here or there, but handling them would still be a mammoth project. Just to be clear, we're not talking about a dozen or so boxes. I recently started to actually catalog the individual volumes with software called "Book Collector." I'm already up to nearly 2,000 items — and that's just doing a few boxes and a few shelves around the edges, not even the main part of the library! I suspect there could be upwards of 3,500 publications and resources here. (Who can believe our feminist/lesbian publishing movement could produce so many vital and energizing collections of words, and art, and ideas!) So, individuals lacking knowledge of lesbian/feminist herstory might potentially just take the whole lot to a donation center, a library book sale, or (heaven forbid) the recycle bin/dumpster.

The thought of transferring these numerous books, journals, newspapers, pamphlets, posters (not many), CDs/tapes, movies, and even a couple of games creates discomfort for me. They are priceless and invaluable to me — a collection overflowing with herstorical meaning, purpose, and identity. I wonder who would care about them. Would younger lesbians/women understand the import of books published by Diana Press, Daughters, Inc., Persephone, Naiad Books, or Kitchen Table/Women of Color Press, and so many others? Would anyone understand the significance of a complete set of the journal called *Lesbian Ethics* or nearly complete sets of *Trivia*, *Sinister Wisdom*, *Common Lives/Lesbian Lives*, *Maize*, and *Hot Wire*? Sadly, I don't know any younger lesbian with the interest or space to take on this collection.

Photograph of Mev Miller's bookshelves featuring lesbian fiction.

Could this library be easily tossed aside as "irrelevant" the way women's artifacts often are? And how much more so because they contain lesbian cultures? [I happen to have a lesbian niece in her thirties who I know could care less about lesbian publications and herstory. Her experiences and lived heteronormative realities as a gay woman are very different than mine have ever been.] Will others regard this library as worthy to treasure or will it be the stuff to create an enormous bonfire to burn heretic witches with their heretic ideas? As I search for a positive happy ending for them – a

Photograph of Mev Miller's bookshelves featuring lesbian journals including *Sinister Wisdom*.

somewhat permanent transfer station – my thoughts and emotions about what to do trip and spiral over and over in anxiety. How much should I care? Does any of this matter, or is it just I being nostalgic longing for the "good-old-days"? Would discarding them equal the discarding of the value of my lesbian identity?

The problem with a private collection is that it's private. What good are these treasures if they sit silently in boxes or on the shelves in all the corners of my house? I take great comfort having those words and visions around me – and many I have yet to read. Though I continue (and need) to re-read them, as I touch each volume, I remember again why I loved them so much in the first place. Wandering over to a shelf to hold and absorb more of Judy Grahn, Audre Lorde, Adrienne Rich, Mary Oliver, Pat Parker, Mary Daly, Cherríe Moraga, Chrystos, Julia Penelope, Barbara Smith, Sally Miller Gearhart, Gloria Anzaldúa, or Paula Gunn Allen – a few of the so, so many wordsmiths – provides great pleasure, comfort, and even fury. But I also know these volumes have generally not been visible or accessible to other lesbians and women who might also enjoy discovering them. Much of what is here has long been out-of-print. Even before their lack of availability, most of these publications could not usually be found in public libraries or even used bookstores (though a casual search now might find some of them on used bookseller websites). These words and ideas have a fuller life when they are shared, discussed, argued about, and celebrated.

Photograph of Mev Miller's bookshelves featuring lesbian non-fiction.

I do have a clear vision for what I would like to do, but making it so will take some planning and probably cost some money. My vision includes a close-to-my-home local library/archive where many of the more readily available volumes could be circulated to any woman/lesbian to borrow and read. (After all, I'd still miss them and would want access to them.) I'm hoping to work in collaboration with the local library system for cataloging and circulation, with the stipulation this specialty library be housed separately and never eliminated. I've already had preliminary discussions with librarians at the local public library as well as a university-based special LGBTQ collection. The volumes that are unique, rare, or tender would stay archived in the location to be visible and enjoyed but kept safe. It's a toss-up for what should happen to the many well-loved books that have my handwritten reflections and comments in the margins. The collection would become a cornerstone to a lesbians/women cultural center, maker space, and community gathering space for enjoying, discussing, sharing, and appreciating lesbians and women's artistic and life-affirming efforts. These publications not only encapsulate lesbian and feminist moments of herstory and culture, but they can continue to live and breathe -- to ignite, inspire, inform, involve, and transform those who read them. As we have always known, we will not be silenced, and our words are powerful.

What happens to all this Lesbiana? Do I trash or treasure? Continue to catalog or leave it alone? Keep to myself or share? Are these volumes destined to be "lost" like so much of our past? Somehow, this extensive collection of lesbian words, ideas – dare I say magic and vision – will be transferred. The questions are why and how and where? I'm curious to know what other lesbian bibliophiles have chosen to do.

Mev Miller: I have lived in Lesbian communities in Detroit, New Haven, Minneapolis/St. Paul, and now Rhode Island. I'm a gardener, writer, editor, photographer, teacher, organizer/activist, collector of Lesbian publications, and singer. As Lesbrarian and Instigator, I'm actively working to establish Wanderground Lesbian Archive/Library. Located in Rhode Island for the New England region, my Lesbiana will provide the cornerstone for a community-based collection. To learn more, visit wanderground.org..

ON MOVING *SINISTER WISDOM* ACROSS THE COUNTRY

A conversation on the transfer of archives with Editor Julie R. Enszer

Julie R. Enszer is the editor and publisher of *Sinister Wisdom*

SM: I remember when I started imagining how this issue on transfer would evolve, you mentioned you had recently moved the **entire** *Sinister Wisdom* archive from California to Florida, where you live, and that the archives become the care of each incoming editor. I knew I had to learn more about the herstory of this process and what it was like for you. Take me through how you came to be the current guardian of the journal's archives and what it was like to inherit the care of such a legacy.

JRE: *Sinister Wisdom* has moved around the United States and the physical archives have been located in different areas, starting with the journal's co-founders', Harriet [Desmoines] and Catherine [Nicholson], house in North Carolina. Then, the archives moved to Montague, MA, Western Massachussets with Michelle [Cliff] and Adrienne [Rich], then moved to Melanie [Kaye/Kantrowitz] and Michaela, initially in Maine. It's very much an itinerant journal.

When I became editor, Susan Levinkind stayed on as the business manager and rented a storage space in Berkeley, California. The back issues were in storage there, and the journal's business operations were headquartered there because Susan and her partner, former *Sinister Wisdom* editor Elana Dykewomon, were based there. They initially kept everything in their house. But it was eventually too much, so they rented a storage space.

Susan became ill with an aggressive form of dementia. She kept managing *Sinister Wisdom* for as long as she could, but then it became clear that she couldn't. I then took over running the database and the subscriptions.

One of the last things that Susan handled was the storage unit in Berkeley. I had never visited it before. In November 2016, we had a great event at the San Francisco Public Library (SFPL) for the Pat Parker Complete Works. My wife and I had *just* moved from Michigan to Florida, and I thought we had space to bring all the books here. I tacked on a couple of days to my California trip for the SFPL event and figured I could ship everything back to my new place in Florida.

We had to cut the locks off the storage unit door because no one could figure out who had the keys to the storage unit. I knew the move was too big of a project for a volunteer to manage, and I didn't know the scope or scale of it. I hired movers and used U-Haul boxes to move it across the country. My friend Irene put her shoulder to the wheel and helped me, and we did it over two days. We packed up 4,000 pounds of books. There was a box or two of papers, but not a lot of what we would consider important.

When I first saw inside the storage unit, it was a "gulp" moment. I didn't have a clear idea of what to do with them. There were 11,000 individual copies of the journal, starting with issue 32 and continuing through 95 - 96. Many were still in the boxes they came in from the printers.

Generally, periodicals have a 6 - 12-month window to sell issues, and then interest wanes. Popular periodicals get pulped (recycled) after just a few months. Specialized periodicals might get specialist interest a bit longer. People are interested now in what is new now and not what was.

Years before, I worked with Cheryl Clarke to distribute back issues of *Conditions* magazine. When I was doing my dissertation research, I asked Cheryl if I could access the archives. She had the full archive of the publication, and it was sitting in storage in New Jersey and had been in storage for twenty years. Her partner is a historian, and every year Cheryl paid the storage unit bill, she said, "Maybe we should get rid of it." Her partner said, "No, that's history, you can't do that." She paid for twenty years to keep that lesbian history.

Cheryl and I distributed 20 - 22 boxes of back issues of *Conditions*. It was not nearly as much as what I had for *Sinister Wisdom*. We initiated a distribution effort, and shipped issues to libraries, including to the Schomburg Center for Research in Black Culture. Now, all I have left is a dozen copies of issue 1 and issue 4. (Those are now gone!)

In retrospect, that experience was a bit of a training wheel period. It informed me of what I was up against when I encountered *Sinister Wisdom*'s Berkeley storage unit. I moved close to 200 boxes from Berkeley to Florida.

It's now been two years since that move happened. We've reduced the back issues by about half. It's reasonable to warehouse between 1,500 and 2,000 back issues. My hope is that the majority of them, such as the Sapphic Classics — which have an ongoing demand for purchase — are saved and in print. I now target my print runs to go out of print after one year. I also convert issues into eBooks, so people can access them, but we don't have to physically store them.

SM: Wow. Did anyone push back on moving the archive from the Bay Area to Florida?

JRE: Not really. When I took over, it became a necessity to move it. And this is in keeping with the tradition of the journal, of course; it moves around. It's not feasible to store 10,000 issues on a regular basis. If you have lived in an urban space, you know that space is at a premium. Now, in Tampa, we have more space, and it's less of an issue.

SM: What would be your ideal scenario for future editors?

JRE: I thought about the future editors after me. It's an entirely volunteer job to be the editor of *Sinister Wisdom*, and you have to warehouse a bedroom's worth of materials. So, assessing the physical storage needs was essential for me. This is part of publishing. This is the big challenge if you're running a literary journal in a place like Los Angeles, New York City, and San Francisco. It's not the same as being in a place like Vermont and

Wisconsin. They say, oh we can put that in a heated room above the barn It's a different

SM: What kinds of considerations are you taking as the current editor of a lesbian publication? What's at stake?

JRE: The papers I have generated since 2010 are going to the Lesbian Herstory Archives [LHA co-founder Joan Nestle is on *Sinister Wisdom*'s board of directors]. I knew Duke Library was interested because of the early papers from Catherine and Harriet. Over time, the journal will have a split archive in this sense. There are papers related to *Sinister Wisdom* in Adrienne Rich's archive at The Arthur and Elizabeth Schlesinger Library on the History of Women in America at Harvard University.

SM: This split archive mirrors the history of the journal in that it's dispersed.

JRE: Right. The work I did editing Pat Parker's book is separated out. Those papers are all at the Schlesinger Library, too. My own work notes and the promotional stuff I kept. At some point, the papers and the books will crush me. It's a constant balance between valuing the history of the journal and not keeping everything and being overwhelmed by the volume of the work.

I plan to be the journal's editor through at least 2026, which is *Sinister Wisdom*'s 50th anniversary. I hope that the only thing the next editor has to do is manage a complete set of the journal. In your questions for the, the issue you're guest editing, *On Transfer* — I think it's also about a balance that ties into the editorial work. How do we hold onto, respect, and enjoy the history while creating the capacious openness we need to imagine the future? I do not want the next editor or future editors to feel so bound and constrained by the past, literally have so much weight to move around, that they don't have enough space for the openness and possibility of the future.

SM: It's about staying visible. That visibility is contingent on the archive being manageable.

JRE: In his book *Archive Fever: A Freudian Impression*, French philosopher Jacques Derrida says we all have a fantasy of going into the archive and creating a history that is thorough. Every archive is like a trail of breadcrumbs: it's never a full meal. The meal needs to come from the reimagination of the past by researchers.

SM: And maybe that's not even the task, to make it complete. That's almost where we get tripped up in academia, is in the task to recreate something accurately. Being ok with it not being everything to everyone. What are your thoughts on the task of holding history?

JRE: The other thing I think about in terms of transfer and the journal is *Sinister Wisdom* and other lesbian journals both consolidate and transfer knowledge and ideas of what it's like to be a lesbian and what it's like to be a lesbian in different times and in different communities. Every issue reflects a different convergence of those communities and ideas.

The journal becomes an object of transference where people imagine a different idea of what lesbian identity means and has meant. Lesbian identity is as contested in our current moment as it was in the past. People often write to me asking if *Sinister Wisdom* is really only a lesbian journal. The answer is that the journal has always had lesbian influence, and that word has meant different things to different editors of the journal and contributors at different times.

There's a lot of women who published in the journal who might not be considered lesbian today. There's a lot of straight women published in the first 25 - 30 issues. When we reach the mid-eighties, the idea of lesbian imagination wanes a little bit. Editors during that period are more interested in writing by lesbians. When Elana Dykewomon became editor, she had a set of lesbian separatist practices that informed her editing. That's the late eighties. Melanie K. acknowledges this in her final letter as an editor of the journal. She had different investments in what lesbian imagination means than Elana. Fran Day, the editor I took over for, was also explicit that every aspect of the journal was created by lesbians. The politics change all the time, with thinking about what do we need right now, so there's an identity politic of the journal that is evolving. My response is, "according to what and when?"

There's so much conversation now around trans lesbians, and I'm thinking about how to create spaces of overlapping investments between lesbians and trans people. People project and transfer a history onto the journal that is often discordant with what's actually in the journal and without a close reading of what the journal actually is and has to say.

Another part of Derrida's *Archive Fever* is a wish to preserve a pure past, but pure is relative to whatever people are seeing now.

SM: Why do you think that is?

JRE: When you live in a place where there are lots of lesbians, you get to draw a line. People weren't interested in drawing lines in Detroit where I started as a writer. The mindset was if you're willing to be out, we're willing to organize with you. Part of me feels like some of these boundary areas are popular with people who are in communities where there are lots of people like them so there can be a richness to dialogue.

Womonwrites has had a painful reckoning with this. I never use TERF as a term. I'm interested in naming people with labels and names they take on. We're in community together, and I have investments in that. I see the realities of the conflicts around us. I think the conflict is generational as well.

SM: Naming as a construct? Why is the term TERF reserved for radical lesbians over sixty?

JRE: I think one reason is that there's an analysis of lesbian feminism that comes out of the eighties. Women with that analysis see gender as a lived-in and embodied experience in the world.

I came out in 1987, in the world of AIDS, and the conversation was very much about being gay and lesbian. Now, it's much more of an alphabet soup world. Different conversations informed then and now.

Another piece is because of misogyny. I don't think we can discount that reality. It's easy to draw lines and harden boundaries and dismiss people you don't have shared experience with.

SM: In efforts to expand definitions of gender and definitions, is there a risk that lesbian-specific culture is being made more invisible?

JRE: I think we have to hold on to the truth we bring. Someone wrote into the journal that "queer erases lesbian." I don't want people to hijack the page. There is an expansiveness of categories, and we know that this does in fact erase specificities. I think about *The Lesbian Continuum* by Adrienne Rich. If everyone is a lesbian, then nobody is a lesbian. People have said that feminism covers up lesbians. Political strategy in labeling things feminist versus lesbian.

I think that's one of the challenges in the lesbian community. How do we have these conversations when our society is so polarized in so many ways and we're invested in enclaves rather than in a large community that has larger conflicts and disagreements? Sarah Schulman in her wonderful book *Conflict Is Not Abuse* outlines many excellent ideas, but there is more work to do. As always.

ANTERIORITY ROSE LIKE BILE

Sarah Werthmann

Anteriority rose like bile
She washed it down with water,
and a smile, like you taught her.

The past felt viscerally present
(the present, noticeably absent)

I never was a good daughter.

Sarah Werthmann is a 26 year-old lesbian living in Portland, Maine

ON BUILDING GENERATIONAL BRIDGES THROUGH CREATIVE COLLABORATIONS

A conversation with Lynn Harris Ballen

Lynn Harris Ballen is the Senior Producer of *Feminist Magazine*, an intersectional radio show/podcast. Born and raised in South Africa, she's a writer and had a career in media and communications ranging from *Los Angeles Magazine* to the L.A. County Natural History Museum. With her late partner and co-conspirator, Jeanne Cordova, she created the queer magazine *Square Peg*, and together they also founded a social justice non-profit in Baja, Mexico. As an LGBTQ and feminist cultural activist, Lynn is passionate about telling untold stories and building coalitions. She's been a longtime lesbian activist in Los Angeles, most recently on the Lambda Litfest founding committee, and is currently the board chair of Dyke Day LA. She's co-produced publications, conferences, and lesbian art/history exhibits including *GenderPlay in Lesbian Culture*, the Lesbian Legacy Wall at ONE Archives, the Butch Voices LA conference, and *Lesbians To Watch Out For: '90s Queer LA Activism*.

Guest Editor's Note: This piece is edited from a 2018 phone interview Susannah Magers did with Lynn Harris Ballen — a conversational Q&A centered on Lynn's creative collaborations and contributions to lesbian and queer culture with her late partner, Jeanne Córdova. Córdova was a Lammy-award winning author, a trailblazer of the lesbian and gay rights movement, a second-wave lesbian feminist activist, founder of iconic publication *The Lesbian Tide*, and a proud butch.

"I hope that the older lesbian feminist generation ... learn that they are not the only definition of lesbians out there. That it was an

era and feminism still lives on, but they need to see what the kids are doing, specifically with their gender and politics. And young people need to see that they didn't just 'pop up' like toast from nowhere — that a lot of people paid a lot, especially in the other generations ... into the forties and fifties, when in the US lesbians were killed for being lesbians. And, we wanted to show them that. That they walk on hallowed ground, that they should feel part of a very long family tree."
— Jeanne Córdova, from a March 2009 *Curve Magazine* article

SM: I wanted to depart from the idea of transfer in relation to intergenerational lesbian culture and LGBTQ archive. What's that balance look like between bringing that material to life and linking all those conversations in a way that's accessible for now? In the queering of everything today, why is naming it and calling it lesbian important?

GenderPlay opening day. Display cases with ephemera from ONE Archives and community members.

Photo Credit: Alice Hom, exhibit designer

LHB: This goes back to early lesbian feminist years — before my time, but it's something I was brought into through Jeanne

— which was the sense that lesbians always fell between the women's movement and the gay movement in the activism sphere. Even now, in intersectional conversations, there's still this sense that you have to choose which of the two spheres you want to operate in more. Lesbians tend to be more forgotten about in the larger LGBTQ acronym, even though the L is at the beginning of that alphabet soup. Jeanne used to say she was never a lesbian separatist, but she was always a lesbian primacist.

SM: Ah, a lesbian primacist — I haven't heard of that term.

Photo Credit: Alice Hom, exhibit designer

From left to right — *GenderPlay* opening day. Title banner; Visitors with interactive Post-it installation.

LHB: She was happy to work with everybody else, to expand all these definitions, and add identities and categories, but she identified as a lesbian and her commitment to the lesbian community was primary. In all the exhibitions and work we did together, there were always broader cultural and community considerations, like when we did *GenderPlay In Lesbian Culture* at the ONE Archives in 2009 — lesbian culture was centered in that exhibition. We refer to the exhibition now as *GenderPlay*.

SM: What you said about the L in LGBTQ — we can't talk about that obscurity, or refusal in some cases, to acknowledge that without talking more broadly about how it's not enough to create intentional space for women. I feel the conversation is often framed around the audacity of claiming space for something specific. I think we run the risk of doing a disservice to the legacy of the lesbian community when we say specificity is no longer relevant just because we've expanded the terminology and the language.

LHB: It came up in all these awards because Jeanne's intention was to claim space, uplift, and affirm lesbians with each of these awards within organizations like Lambda Literary, The National Gay and Lesbian Journalists Association, with Astraea as well. We got feedback from folks around eligibility to apply, so we expanded the language.

After the performances at the *GenderPlay* exhibition opening event. From left to right: Jeanne Cordova, Marie Cartier, Phranc, and Lynn Ballen. From Lynn: "Phranc and Marie both performed — the audience was so big that we were breaking fire marshall laws, so Jeanne asked all the performers to do a second show!".

Photo Credit: Angela Brinskele

SM: How do you feel about that?

LHB: As long as we're still within the spirit of lesbian-first in those wordings, I'm ok with it. I'm aware that there are trans women who identify as lesbian, and they qualify. To me, broadening lesbian identity and expanding the definition of women is feminist at its core. I was comfortable with that as long as we stayed within the spirit of what's intended — to celebrate lesbians. When we did the Butch Voices LA conference, we wanted to make sure that everyone felt welcome, so we just gathered all these words and made a word cloud on a postcard. If you are any of these things broadly under the umbrella, you're welcome to join us, but the primary word is butch. That exercise in language expansion is the intention, right?

SM: Yes. Expanding the definition of women resonates with me. That's probably one of the more succinct, compelling phrasings of that idea: you can be a part of this club, but here are the conditions. You're opening up what that is while still advocating for specificity.

LHB: I think it's not about conditions for entry, but more about keeping lesbians at the center, instead of checking the boxes of how you're supposed to fit into the traditional gender roles. And for non-binary dykes, that means rejecting the gender binary altogether.

SM: What are some of the bridges that you have built, or have seen built, around making these intergenerational connections that prioritize lesbian culture, resources, archives, experience? What are some bridges that you think still need to be built?

LHB: Hmm, good question. Jeanne and I moved to Mexico for almost ten years. When we moved back to LA, we realized we had changed, and we had this intention to work differently and create different projects and connections. It's almost like you see something from the outside, coming back into it, and we realized there were multiple generations doing different work simultaneously, at least three out generations. I think it started with Yolanda Retter, a librarian and archivist who was really convincing Jeanne to sort her archives and her collection and find a home for it while she was still alive, rather than doing it after her, so she could name and categorize everything, and particularly the context for all the photos and documents and everything.

Yolanda was sort of a maverick, and she and Jeanne had been kind of frenemies for many years — I think it was a case of dating the same women. And Yolanda was just this character: she had all these names and categories for herself, like she was a gadfly on the lesbian body politic. She was a knight for higher. She worked at both the Mazer Archives and the ONE Archives, and she ended up running the Chicano resource library at UCLA. She was my mentor in understanding what archives did and what was needed.

Yolanda told a cautionary tale of sorting a collection of photos that were categorized by somebody who wasn't queer or Latino. One photo had been labeled as "Gay men getting off a boat on a beach in Florida." She looked at it, saw the context, got the dates, and realized that the photo was of the Mariel Boatlift. Fidel Castro had expelled gay men who had been imprisoned, and this photo was of that group of gay men. So, she really impressed upon us how important it was for somebody from the culture, from your subculture and community, to be the person who was categorizing and naming what was in the collection — how vital that was. That's why it was so important to her that Jeanne processed her own collection.

SM: Wow. What a powerful story.

LHB: Only about 80% of the collection was done before Jeanne passed. I still have about 20% to do. That story always resonated for me. I've experienced that since. I've been to, um, I think it was a, um, a collection's launch at UCLA where it was, you know, somebody who wasn't from the community was miscategorizing or missing something so badly. And it was just — I could see how frustrating and, and, and how our history can be lost. For me, the importance of the cross-generational engagement and transfer is this concept that — and I don't have a word for it — of how we are not necessarily born into queer, lesbian, or gay families, unlike any other minority groups. If you're Black or Latinx, for example, you're born into a family that passes along culture that might otherwise be erased and teaches you how to survive oppression — "the talk." Queer people don't often have that. I saw Hannah Gadsby's one woman show, *Nanette*, live last night. She's astonishing. She talks about the depth of pain and shame; that, as a queer person, you can be soaked in homophobia in your family and your small town, in Tasmania, in Australia, rather than having your identity affirmed. I feel, and Jeanne felt, deeply, that we are the queer or lesbian parents of the next generation. We have to then pass on the stories. It's that grandmothering and mothering and parenting concept of the family stories. We have to pass them along to the next generation because otherwise the dominant culture is just gonna wipe them out. Michelangelo Signorile talks about this more politically. I just feel very passionately about that.

After *GenderPlay* opening, most of the LEXbians who put the exhibit together celebrated at the French Quarter Restaurant (a favorite queer activist gathering place).

SM: That's transference: taking on this responsibility, to be a mirror, a reference point, or a role model.

LHB: Exactly. I follow a lot of wonderful accounts on Instagram, and I see the connection to elders and ancestors. There's a more automatic connection there, but we as lesbians and queers have to actively create that connection.

SM: I couldn't agree more.

LHB: I come from a magazine and publishing background; I'm a writer. I've worked on exhibitions, conferences, and subcultural projects. I would go out, find folks that we want to work with, and build a team in that way. That's how I began the LEX project with Jeanne. We put the word out, asked who wanted to work on this, but we also actively invited artists, filmmakers, and activists that we wanted to work with, too. We purposely incorporated three generations — LA has folks from all kinds of backgrounds, and it was important to us to include as many diverse perspectives as possible. We decided we didn't want to make it formal; we thought of starting a nonprofit at one point, and then we thought, no, we'd rather just do the work when we're inspired — a guerrilla-style, pop-up group. We'd work with the ONE Archives, or the City of West Hollywood, different fiscal sponsors. The bridge-building was from the beginning instead of sort of creating something with, like, just people who were like you and then bringing in other folks and other perspectives after the event was already shaped. We always had tons of committee meetings — the broad representation of points of view was already there.

SM: You were thinking and acting with intersectionality in mind.

LHB: And in an intentionally feminist way. I wouldn't call us a collective, but it was sort of a loose collective, though the word *collective* signals for me a necessity for consensus, and consensus is so painful when you're doing something creative and on a deadline. When we did Jeanne's memorial, and it was kind of a highly produced project, I emailed the Lexbians — we called ourselves the Lexbians.

SM: I like that. And, of course, the "x" within language now is a way to denote the plural, being queer.

LHB: Exactly! I emailed the Lexbian crew and asked, "Who wants to help?" And they all showed up, with sound and cameras and visuals and hammers and tools, tools. Everybody that had been on our creative team that had done exhibits and conferences. We all knew how to work with each other; it was just such a loving gift. It's very intentional bridge-building.

SM: I want to return to thinking about ways to make archival materials accessible, that isn't holding a manuscript carefully with gloves. There's other ways that people need to experience this.

LHB: Right. I mean, the preciousness of queer archives, and perhaps the reticence to work intergenerationally, comes from a generation who experienced a level of persecution and oppression, that makes them fear their culture will be erased. But we need to accept that we're in a new paradigm. Even though we're not living in a perfect world free of homophobia, we've now got more generations that are visible. And, in fact, we will protect our culture even more by sharing all of this with our queer children.

SM: Creating other stewards of queer legacies.

LHB: Jeanne did a panel discussion with the Mazer Archive about all of the women's centers in LA. When the original Westside Women's Center building closed, Jeanne saved and stored the red and black sign in her garage. She kept it, and when they reopened, she wanted to present it back to the archive. She knew it needed to be preserved in the Mazer Archives. So, we organized a panel discussion with all the founders of all these different women's spaces from the mid- to late-seventies. The first Los Angeles women's shelter was founded by lesbians.

SM: I didn't know that!

LHB: Jeanne had been on the board of the ONE Archives in the early nineties, and it was a difficult time. There was a lot of infighting between an earlier generation of older gay men who had saved and preserved all these collections who didn't want to grow and expand and were understandably suspicious of the possibility of the archive being a part of USC. I remember when we moved back from Mexico and walked into the building, we saw this wall of all the ONE magazine covers, and they're visually gorgeous, but there's literally two that had the word lesbian on them.

SM: I noticed that, too, when I first visited the ONE Archives.

LHB: We proposed a lesbian publications wall, and we displayed covers from 1948 to 2008. We started with original copies of *Vice Versa*, the first known lesbian publication in North America. The last one was a screenshot of *After Ellen* because we were like, here's where lesbian publications are going — onto the web. We had an artist create what was supposed to be a spiral. We actually tracked down Lisa Ben, the creator of *Vice Versa*. People had sort of forgotten her, that she was still alive. We found her and brought her to the event to be honored. Judy Grahn came, a bunch of *The Lesbian Tide* folks came — all appeared and spoke. Phranc told stories and, yeah, it was a really cool launch event. Jeanne shared why folks should give their collections during their lives and why it matters that we give our collections to our own institutions rather than to places like the Smithsonian. The Women's Building gave stuff to the Smithsonian and then evidently it got damaged in a basement tragically.

SM: Oh no! That's horrible.

LHB: The events and exhibits always have an activist aspect to them. In 2017, I co-curated an exhibit called *Lesbians to Watch Out For: '90s Queer L.A. Activism* with longtime activist Judy Sisneros. We worked with a broader group inspired by, and working with, nineties activists — members of ACT UP, Queer Nation and the Lesbian Avengers — and we invited younger gen activists in to be part of the research and writing as well.

SM: I'm thinking about the legacy of LEX. Do you have a website or an archive for that project specifically?

LHB: I should! There's a website for Butch Voices LA, but it's down because there's some kind of malware and, um, and I've just never gotten around to fixing it. LEX does deserve an archive website.

SM: There's so many people that are doing this everyday archival work all the time, even if it's not in a recognized mainstream way. In our own way, we're all doing this. This conversation right now is part of that.

Archival materials for *Lesbians to Watch Out For* exhibit. Planning meetings at Lynn's dining room table!

LHB: Right. When we did *Lesbians to Watch Out For* last year, it was fascinating to me because I had a bunch of nineties material, but Judy Sisneros, the co-curator, had *so* much material because she was a part of ACT UP and Queer Nation, involved in the queer and punk music scene, and she's also a photographer. When we put the word out for photos, flyers, and t-shirts, I cleared out a spare bedroom in my house, and people brought all this stuff! The original inspiration for the exhibit came out of the fact that it was the Lesbian Avengers' 25th anniversary, and we were invited to exhibit their anniversary banners, but there had not been a chapter in LA. So, we started looking at all of the direct action and grassroots organizing by lesbians in LA in addition to Queer Nation and ACT UP: Puss in Boots, which was a brief group, the LA Dyke March. We also wanted to ensure that lesbian of color nineties organizing groups were included, like United Lesbians of African Heritage (ULOAH) and Los Angeles Asian Pacific Islander Sisters (LAAPIS), so we reached out to friends who had been involved. I was literally asking folks to gather their friends and then sitting in people's living rooms persuading them to lend me their materials for the show. We were doing primary research. We had not planned to do that, but that's how it turned out.

SM: I think that's an important aspect of it. Going back to this intergenerational bridge idea, what were some of the responses or critical feedback that you got to *Lesbian to Watch Out For*?

LHB: During the process of creating the exhibition, finding the core people required a lot of networking with other communities: what was bisexual and trans women's organizing history? Nobody remembered where key people in these movements were; maybe one person had an old email for a contact, and you had to track them down. For example, I found out about LAAPIS (Los Angeles Asian Pacific Islander Sisters) through a dear friend who was a very early API lesbian organizer in the Bay Area, but she lives in LA now. She vouched for me and all of these API dykes, none of whom knew me well, were sitting in my friend's living room. They were holding boxes of personal ephemera, and the pain of the memories of what it took to organize as a community was palpable; they were clearly going through that trauma again. Is it safe for them, through these materials, to be out in the world? The answer to that question was processed in an afternoon. That was quite a remarkable experience.

SM: A lot of trust is required when thinking about who we tell our stories to.

LHB: It only worked because of a mutual friend who vouched for me. It was understandably like, who are you, you white woman? They were telling each other stories and remembering, and it was very clear that they weren't even sure what it would feel like for them to have their stories, photos, and lives to be public. How to walk them through that, you know? A sad story from this experience of gathering stories and materials for *Lesbian to Watch Out For* (*LTWOF*) is that Yolanda had gathered all of this material, and a lot of people's collections are with the Chicano Resource Center at UCLA, such as Lesbianas Unidas, but they haven't been processed, so we could not access a lot of the material because we didn't know what was where. That really broke my heart because ten years later, even after Yolanda was instrumental in getting our materials processed, and it so was important. We've talked about fundraising to get the Lesbianas Unidas collection and others that are sitting there processed.

SM: Such a vulnerable process to literally hand over your history to someone else.

LHB: It is. And as much as people are reluctant to share their collections and lives publicly, there's also frustration from those who want to be included but feel they haven't been. For example, we did three public events for *Lesbians to Watch Out For*. At the panel discussion event, women who had been involved in more mainstream organizations in nineties LA asked why they weren't included in the exhibit. They argued their organizations and work were key parts of this history. I explained that we decided to focus on the untold stories of direct action, street activism, and grassroots organizing. So, if you had an office, and a board of directors, your history has already been told somewhere.

SM: Good for you. That's a really practical response. I can understand where they're coming from, wanting to be included. But part of the work of curating is you have to edit and focus and sometimes people get hurt if they're not incorporated. All you can do is share your methodology — and it doesn't negate them or their contribution to the larger community and narrative.

LHB: There had been tension between their organizations and those like Queer Nation. For example, we included the Hollywood Homophobia campaign in the exhibition — Queer Nation took an opposing side to GLAAD. The GLAAD co-founders kept saying, well, GLAAD started as grassroots because we started in someone's living room. I said, yeah, but that doesn't qualify you as grassroots per se. GLAAD's approach was to come from a more reformist, institutional place; they wanted to be into dialogue with the powers that be. There were big disagreements over how to situate key lesbian characters in mainstream media and movies. GLAAD consulted with the producers of *Fried Green Tomatoes* — that was the most difficult one to reconcile. Yeah. Because GLAAD worked with the producers on that one. It was considered a progressive film, and GLAAD was completely supportive of the film. But, the way the script ended up written, the overt lesbianism of the characters in the book was whitewashed in the film. Hollywood Homophobia protested the film because of this, so there was this clear line between them and GLAAD — it was what we used to call in the nineties "suits versus streets."

Lesbians To Watch Out For closing night. Some of the team who researched and created the exhibition.

SM: It was a critical response, and rightly so! Were there women from the younger generations who said, wow, I didn't know that this existed — what intergenerational feedback did the *Lesbians to Watch Out For* exhibition receive?

Lesbians To Watch Out For, opening night.
Co-curators Lynn Harris Ballen and Judy Sisneros
with activists who were featured in the exhibit.

LHB: Yes, we got a lot of folks who had lived through the nineties and were reliving their memories, finding themselves in photos and having lovely emotional flashbacks. There were a lot of younger generations who came through and were amazed. The show opened during Pride month, part of a West Hollywood-sponsored month of programming called One City, One Pride. They gave us funding and gallery space. After that month, this young professor from a small private university in the San Gabriel Valley, The University of La Verne, which was originally a Christian university. She did her primary research on the Lesbian Avengers. She asked if she could bring the exhibition to the university. And then we were reaching a new audience, many of whom were first-generation to go to college. They were drawn to the visuals and seeing themselves, posing and taking selfies next to the ULOAH wall panel, and the API organizations wall panel. They were finding themselves in there. That was really wonderful.

THE LESBIAN TIDE
OCT. 1973
50¢ in L. A. Area
65¢ Elsewhere
A FEMINIST PUBLICATION, WRITTEN BY AND FOR THE RISING TIDE OF WOMEN TODAY

N. Y. SAPPHASAURA

Photo Credit: *The Lesbian Tide*

The Lesbian Tide reported on lesbian stories everywhere. This is a cover story by East Coast Correspondent Karla Jay about the Sapphasaura, a paper mache lavender dinosaur that Lesbian Feminist Liberation created to march up Central Park West to protest the American National History Museum in 1973.

We finalized another tour of *Lesbians to Watch Out For* [in 2019]. One stop is at Cal State Los Angeles, in their main library, which is kind of amazing. This connection happened through a professor who approached us who teaches in their woman, gender, and sexuality studies specialty. They're going to do programming, and I'm interested to see how everyone responds.

Cover of the August 1974 issue of The Lesbian Tide.

SM: That's so exciting. Congratulations! The work is continuing to live on. In addition to the re-presentation of the show you just mentioned, what are some other projects you have in the works or that you're excited about that are generational calls to action?

LHB: I'm very excited about all of the LGBT history accounts that are bringing the history alive for the next generation. I started doing an informal Flashback Friday for *The Lesbian Tide*. *Autostraddle* does a lesbian, bi, and queer summer camp. They were one of Jeanne's trust beneficiaries because she wanted to support a magazine that she thought was the next generation of *The Lesbian Tide* in a way. They wrote an exquisite feature and thank you to Jeanne that she had written so honestly about the personal and financial struggles of keeping something going like *The Tide*. *Autostraddle* sent me an email yesterday with a photo — evidently each cabin had a banner with a name on it, and they had, like, a *Lesbian Tide* cabin.

Butch Voices LA organizers and volunteers packing up at the end of the weekend (with a U-Haul of course!).

SM: How cool!

LHB: A big part of how we set up Jeanne's trust, awards, scholarships, and gifts is to be intentionally cross-generational. To answer your question, I've considered a revival of *Gender Play* to add — not modify, but add — to how much things have shifted in the generational conversation on gender. It feels like it would probably be really difficult, but at the same time really interesting, because the show debuted in 2009. So much has changed in the ten years since. For me, that exhibit was visually the most beautiful one. We had an amazing designer for that one.

SM: What advice would you give to lesbian-identified creative and art makers working now?

LHB: The biggest piece of advice would be to work communally. To build your team with that in mind. I find that in my personal writing work and with *The Feminist Magazine KPFK* radio show and podcast that I produce and co-host. I grew up as an only child, but I have two brothers because I was adopted, and I traced my biological family, and I have this lovely family situation now, I've had them for, like, twenty-eight years. But for the first half of my life, I was an only child.

Jeanne, on the other hand, came from a family of twelve children and to her, you didn't do anything alone, you know? Jeanne always formed a group to do *everything*. She was perfectly conditioned already for lesbian feminism and collective ways of working. I really learned that from her — you form your own group. I host this writing group called Lezerati. We meet every two weeks to critique, give feedback, and support each other's work. These are lesbian groups, and it's always this kind of support and enrichment that catalyzes and makes your work more and better — it all happens in those collective spaces.

INSTALLATION IMAGES FROM
POLITICAL BIRTHDAYS

Susannah Magers

Political Birthdays was a 2018 group exhibition inspired by the words of Jeanne Córdova. Curated by Susannah Magers, the exhibition was on view in the fall of 2018 at Dream Farm Commons in downtown Oakland, California. **The title, *Political Birthdays*, is an homage to a quote by the late founder of *The Lesbian Tide*, activist, organizer, publisher, and writer Jeanne Córdova.** In Gregorio Davila's 2017 film, *Jeanne Córdova: Butches, Lies, and Feminism*, Córdova recalls when she discovered the Daughters of Bilitis (one of the first lesbian civil and political rights organizations in the United States) and describes this as her "political birthday," a moment of recognition and surfacing of her passion and dedication to social justice, civil rights, and community organizing.

In this spirit, *Political Birthdays* contemplated how we can support each other in the face of divisiveness and uncertainty, and how the space of the exhibition can engender a call to action and inhabit both critical and celebratory modalities in this regard.

Composed of video, performance ephemera, flags, textiles, painting, mixed-media, Risograph posters, fabric, sculpture, and works on paper, the exhibition emphasized visibility, agency, and collaboration as resources, sites of inquiry, and tools. The works in *Political Birthdays* leverage sculptural forms, language, patterns, color, text, and texture as political signifiers that inhabit and perform a kind of coded visibility. Taking up themes ranging from immigration, sexuality, and social justice, to identity, resilience, and marginality, each artist employs strategic and symbolic visual and conceptual devices that reframe and reflect back intentional, intersectional aims.

Participating artists: Anna Luisa Petrisko (Los Angeles, CA); Artemisa Clark (Los Angeles, CA); Grace Rosario Perkins (Albuquerque, NM); Jessalyn Aaland (Oakland, CA); Mary Tremonte (Pittsburgh, PA and Toronto, ON); Lukaza Branfman-Verissimo (Oakland, CA); Mary Beth Magyar (Rochester, MN); Sarah Hotchkiss (San Francisco, CA); Weird Allan Kaprow (Portland, OR); Virginia Broersma (Long Beach, CA); Christine Wong Yap (Queens, NY).

Photo Credit: Susannah Magers

View of the 2018 group exhibition *Political Birthdays* from the sidewalk outside of Oakland project space Dream Farm Commons. Artwork in windows from right: Lukaza Branfman-Verissimo, *Listen to Bright Anger*, *Listen to Bright Sweet Anger*, 2018. Tumeric dyed cotton, paint, grommets, printed recipe, flags, performance documentation Dimensions variable; Christine Wong Yap, *Irrational Exuberance Flag #6*, 2012. Fabric, thread, grommets, 48 x 80 inches.

Installation views of *Political Birthdays*. From right: Lukaza Branfman-Verissimo. *Listen to Bright Anger, Listen to Bright Sweet Anger*, 2018; Mary Beth Magyar. *Disclose*, 2018; Jessalyn Aaland *Class Set Volume 1*, 2017.

Photo Credit: Susannah Magers

Installation views of *Political Birthdays*. Left and right images: Grace Rosario Perkins, *Agency*, 2018. Acrylic on paper; Weird Allan Kaprow, *Self-Karaoke*, 2018. Eight videos with music and karaoke lyrics massage chair, iPad, audio, song book. Christine Wong Ya, *Irrational Exuberance Flag # 3*, 2012 (in back, in window) Fabric, thread, grommets; *Irrational Exuberance Flag # 6*, 2012 (in front, in window).

From left: Mary Tremonte, *Born in Flames*, 2016; Four color hand-silkscreened print signed and numbered edition of 50; Mary Tremonte, Four screen-printed fabric bandanas with raccoon, otter, beaver, and wolf prints, 2018 Hand-printed on pre-sized 100% cotton bandanas; Anna Luisa Petrisko, *Jeepneys* bodysuit from experimental opera performance, *Bumbayaya*, 2012 Paint, spandex bodysuit.

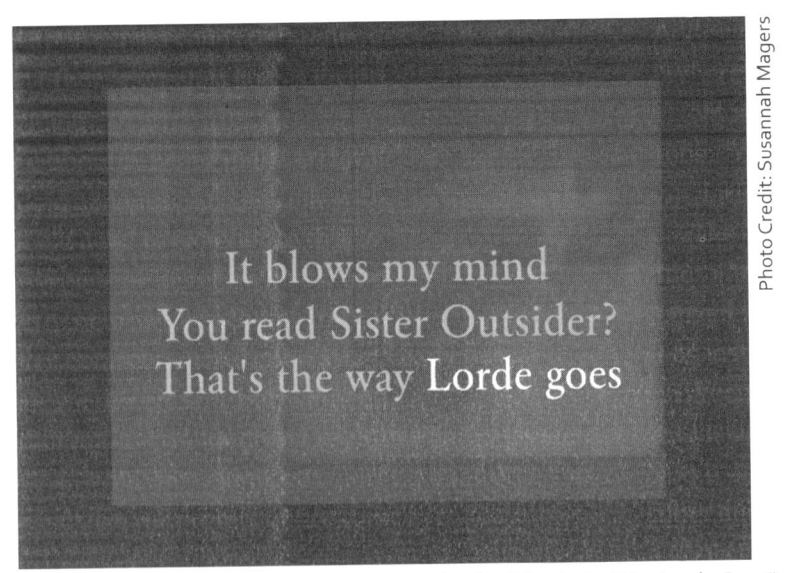

> It blows my mind
> You read Sister Outsider?
> That's the way **Lorde goes**

Screenshot of video accompanying music video for "That's the Way Lorde Goes" (to the tune of "That's the Way Love Goes" by Janet Jackson).

New Lesbian Writing

THE KITTIWAKE

Bronwyn Hughes

When the pandemic struck, the office at Whitman's Marina shuttered overnight, marooning the liveaboards on Sandy Bottom Creek like a lost colony. Onboard the Kittiwake, Fran cradled her partner's wasted body, pleading with Jackie to come back, to tell her how to handle this. As the afternoon passed, light rippled across the low ceiling, moving from the bow hatch to the bilge pump. Fran's shallow breathing gradually deepened. At sunset, she kissed Jackie's forehead and rose to call her daughter.

The still water surrounding Whitman's Marina gleamed metallic, like a bead of mercury. Mud clung to the soles of Fran's red Topsiders after she traipsed across the boatyard to find a working pay phone. She removed her shoes and placed them in a bin on the Kittiwake's portside deck. Inside, she leaned against the pilothouse door until the lock mechanism clicked, then tugged once more at the stubborn half-inch gap between the curtains.

"Alice is on her way," Fran said, lifting her voice toward Jackie's body in the sleeping quarters. She no longer expected a response, but she wasn't ready to end their twenty-year-long conversation yet. "Alice says it's a twelve-hour drive from Quebec to Virginia, so she should arrive here by daybreak. I begged her not to drive at night. 'What's your rush,' I said, 'Jackie's already dead.' But she never listens to me."

Stepping down a wooden ladder into the galley, Fran clicked on the propane burner to heat water. "Want some of my tea, Jackie? We're out of your chai." Fran began to hum a tune by the McGarrigle sisters that reminded her of a time before she and Jackie met.

"I know you and Alice don't always see eye to eye. You're both so headstrong — but look how much she cares about you. She's driving all night for you." Fran chuckled. "Remember the time Alice's boys came aboard? You took us to that dive site with the sunken ship near Isle La Motte? You really are good with children, Jackie. You just need more patience."

The tea kettle whistled. Fran poured herself a cup of mandarin orange oolong. She sat at the dinette with her socks on the cushion and her knees folded like a grasshopper to keep warm. The thermostat in the pilothouse read seventy-eight degrees, but Fran was always cold.

"Alice says they still have two feet of snow on the ground up there. I told her she won't need her winter parka down here. The azaleas are starting to bloom."

That reminded Fran to throw away the dried-up daffodils and forsythia Lorraine had left on the dock beside the Kittiwake when she heard Jackie had COVID-19 symptoms two weeks ago. Fran had removed the rubber band and newspaper wrapping from the stems and placed the flowers in a mason jar on the dinette, setting aside the newspaper to read later.

Lorraine kept the books at Whitman's Marina. Over the twenty years that Fran and Jackie had lived on the Kittiwake, Lorraine was Fran's only real friend besides Jackie. Fran looked forward to returning to Whitman's each fall so she could resume their friendship until April, when Jackie would begin preparations to sail back north to Lake Champlain for the summer. When news of coronavirus first flooded the marine radio waves, Jackie insisted that the pandemic wouldn't make any difference to their daily lives. Never liking to admit she was wrong, Jackie fumed when she saw how fast Lorraine closed the office and stopped coming to the marina. Fran decided not to show Jackie the prayer card for healing that Lorraine had taped to the flower wrapping. Jackie needed her strength to fight the virus.

"Alice will have to drive through New York to get down here, won't she?" Having grown up in Quebec, Fran's knowledge of America's overland geography was still poor.

She tapped her chipped, red-painted fingernail against a headline from the newspaper wrapping. "Says here they're burying people in mass graves in New York City because funeral directors are overwhelmed." Fran removed her reading glasses and rubbed her bloodshot eyes. "Alice will call the authorities when she gets here and tangle everything up. How did I raise such a conformist? If I don't figure something out, there won't be a thing I can do to stop her."

Fran reached across the helm for her cigarettes and lit one using the lighter that hung by a string over the nautical charts. In her attempt to get Jackie to eat something, she had forgotten to feed herself for the past few days. One of the liveaboards at Whitman's had suggested she try giving Jackie some of those calorie-filled milkshakes to build her strength, so she had taken the marina's beach bike into town and filled her backpack with cans of Ensure from the grocery store. All but one remained unopened next to the stove in the galley. Even though Jackie was too weak to eat, she had refused to go to the hospital. She had a deep distrust of doctors.

The marine radio in the pilothouse squawked with the Coast Guard performing evening drills. Jackie had always monitored channel sixteen for offshore distress calls and channel sixty-eight for local correspondence around Sandy Bottom Creek, in case she could assist in an emergency. The marine radio broadcast was the only news she cared about.

"Do you think the Americans will try to stop Alice from crossing the border? If anyone can get through, it's Alice." Fran smiled. "My pretty blond pit bull. She'll tell them her mother's partner died. Maybe she should say 'stepparent' instead of 'mother's partner' to make it sound more urgent, don't you think? But I guess she can't, since we never legally married."

Fran scratched her head through her knitted beanie. She rarely took it off, even to sleep. She liked the way it contained her frizzy gray hair, which began to escape the longer she put off a haircut.

Small and thin, she wore red leggings, which made her look even more like a kittiwake, the red-legged shore bird their boat was named for. They chose the name when they decided to follow the kittiwake's migration pattern, wintering in Virginia and summering on Lake Champlain between Vermont and Canada.

When Fran met Jackie at the Hertz rental car office in Burlington, Vermont, they were both middle-aged, wearing bright yellow customer service blazers. Fran smiled at Jackie from across the break room because Jackie seemed so uncomfortable. The short, spiky haircut and set jaw told Fran that Jackie wasn't cut out for hospitality. Assigned to train her, Fran quickly realized Jackie wasn't trainable. Two weeks later, after the manager fired Jackie, Fran quit so they could sail away together on Jackie's boat.

Fran picked up the prayer for healing card from Lorraine and let her mind wander back to Saint-Jean-sur-Richelieu, where she grew up. The nuns at her parochial school seemed so free from indecision that she briefly considered joining a convent before she got pregnant with Alice. Why hadn't she and Lorraine ever discussed religion, she wondered. *Had Lorraine secretly disapproved of her relationship with Jackie?*

"After I finish this cup of tea, Jackie, we're going to clean you up. I'm going to put you in your Indigo Girls T-shirt and a fresh pair of jeans — just like you're going to a womyn's music festival."

Struggling to get Jackie's bony legs into her Levi's, Fran worried Jackie's pants would slide off when someone came to move her because her body had shriveled so much in the past few days. Even the last notch on her belt wasn't tight enough to make a difference. Fran pulled out her sewing kit from under her berth and used cloth-cutting scissors to remove a pizza-slice section of denim. Then she forced a needle back and forth through the thick fabric until Jackie's jeans fit snugly on her hips.

After Fran sponged Jackie's face and neck, she noticed her fingernails needed clipping. Jackie's hair seemed to have grown more than usual since Fran had last cut it. Afraid of pulling too hard on Jackie's scalp, she gently trimmed and straightened her silver bangs.

"Hold still," she instructed as she tweezed Jackie's chin.

Looking her over, something was missing. She had forgotten Jackie's glasses, which were folded in the cubby next to Mary Oliver's *Upstream*, the book of essays she was reading before she fell into a coma. Jackie had consulted Mary Oliver's poems throughout their relationship, so Fran tucked it under Jackie's arm. She wiped the lenses and placed Jackie's glasses back on her face. *Shoes, or no shoes?* She knew Jackie always preferred to go barefoot, but Fran decided to pull socks over her feet anyway and wrestle on her L.L. Bean duck boots. As a final touch, Fran slipped Jackie's Swiss Army knife and her "One Day at a Time" AA coin in her front pocket.

Satisfied that Jackie was ready for viewing, Fran picked up the VHF handset and tuned the radio to channel sixty-eight to transmit her message that Captain Jackie's time had come. Sandy Bottom Creek, where the river met the Chesapeake Bay, hosted some of Mobjack, Virginia's most expensive yachts alongside some of its most humble vessels. She invited the nocturnal liveaboards on the Creek to pay their last respects.

Placing the handset back in its cradle, she wondered if anyone would come, or if — like Lorraine — they would be afraid of catching the virus. Without submitting to a test, Jackie declared she had the flu, not coronavirus. Fran never questioned Jackie. When the Kittiwake was underway, their mutual survival depended on a clear chain of command.

Fran peeked through the gap in the curtains to see if the "fellas," as Jackie referred to her rogue band of friends, would emerge from their floating shanties to answer her radio call. No longer seaworthy, most of their vessels were permanently moored, like a decaying reef. The liveaboards socialized by skittering around the creek in their dinghy boats at night after the day cruisers went home. Many nights, Fran fell asleep listening to Captain Jackie argue her philosophical and political views with a group of drunken fellas gathered at the end of the pier. Jackie was the only female in the group, except for a hooker named Wonder Woman.

To Fran's relief, the sound of outboard motors and the smell of exhaust began to pervade the creek as twenty or more skiffs converged on the Kittiwake.

"Permission to come aboard?" the first to arrive asked.

Fran sat in Jackie's captain's chair, swiveling to welcome them aboard and gesturing toward the sleeping quarters for viewing. Fran could smell that most of them had been drinking all day. She felt grateful to have met Jackie after she got sober. Jackie never swallowed a drop during their twenty years together. But because of her boozy past, she had always helped the fellas when they got into drunken scrapes.

The men stepped aboard gingerly, afraid to track any sort of disrespect into Fran's home. Soon their timidity gave way to shouting, each vying to tell Fran their story of how Captain Jackie had helped them out of a worse bind.

"I'll never forget how Cap'n Jackie towed me off that sandbar," a fella with kind eyes said. "I didn't know who else to call."

Another leaned in to confess, "Cap'n Jackie posted my bail — then she helped me apply for my Trump relief check to pay my court fees."

One with spider tattoos covering his neck gave Fran a wooden carving of a kittiwake he had whittled when he heard Jackie was sick.

Last to arrive were two young guys and a three-legged hound dog. They tied up their skiff in an empty slip and made their way over the wooden docks that crisscrossed the marina like lattice. Fran watched them approach as the men onboard passed out Dixie cups and began toasting Captain Jackie with shots of Wild Turkey.

"Do you remember us, ma'am? We're the Foster brothers. I'm Willis and this is Hotdog. We owe our lives to Cap'n Jackie for the time our boat caught fire."

Fran recognized them, and their old dog sitting outside. Hotdog had taken his baseball cap off out of respect, revealing burn scars on the left side of his scalp, ear, and face.

"If you ever need *anything*, ma'am, you call us. Anything at all."

"*Anything?*" This was the first word Fran had spoken since her radio call.

Willis looked her deep in the eyes. "Me and Hotdog got you covered."

Everyone quieted to listen to a raspy-voiced fella with a guitar sing Jackie's favorite John Prine song. In the serenity of the moment, a simple solution came to Fran, as if Jackie herself had whispered in her ear. With a quickening pulse, her eyes darted around the room, courage rising from her abdomen.

"One more song," she called before ushering the men off the Kittiwake—all but the Foster brothers. She had to hurry. Alice would be here in a few hours.

*

Two hours later, when the tide peaked, Fran stood on the stern of the Kittiwake wrapped in a blanket she had crocheted for Jackie, watching the Foster brothers motor away in their skiff to fulfill her wish. She lost sight of their running lights when they cleared the jetty and turned hard to port toward deep water. After their watery trail stilled, she went back inside, pulled her knees to her chest, and removed her beanie. Her blue eyes sparkled as tears traced the ruts of her tanned, leathery cheeks.

The clock in the pilothouse chimed four, reminding her that Alice would arrive soon. Jackie's belongings — her captain's log, her waders hanging on a hook, her bird-watching binoculars, her Christmas cactus — all seemed flat now, like brushstrokes on a canvas. Fran's tiny still-life of a home felt fragile. She drifted to sleep, satisfied she had not let Jackie down.

*

Static on the VHF radio roused Fran at daybreak as watermen on the Chesapeake motored down the creek to set their crab floats. She opened the curtains wide and squinted at the red sunrise over the bow. *Red sky at night, sailors delight; red sky in the morning, sailors take warning.* She stepped outside to loosen the spring lines.

Looking up, she saw Alice's white SUV, covered with splatter from the long drive, rolling into the marina's gravel parking area. Watching Alice get out of the car and stretch, Fran startled at the sight of her daughter in a surgical mask. Fran approached for a hug, but Alice backed away.

"Careful, Mom. You're contagious, and I can't afford to get sick. I need to keep a safe distance from you."

"Nonsense! I'm your mother. Come aboard and I'll make you a cup of coffee."

"Mom, I can't set foot on your boat or get anywhere near Jackie's body. You don't seem to understand how contagious this virus is."

"If it's so contagious, why don't I have it? Jackie started feeling sick two weeks ago."

"I don't know. Maybe you're asymptomatic."

Alice had twisted her blond hair into a messy bun for the drive. She wore no makeup or jewelry. Her floppy McGill sweatshirt hung almost to her knees over leggings tucked into Uggs. Fran thought she looked prettier like this than when she wore a power suit and pumps for her downtown lawyer job.

Alice took out her iPhone and told Siri to find the number for a funeral home near here. Fran listened to her daughter's side of the conversation.

"Not sure. Hang on — Mom, has anyone pronounced Jackie dead yet?"

"She's dead. There, I just did."

"No," Alice said, turning away from her mother. "No address either. The deceased lived on a boat at…" She glanced around until she saw faded lettering across the back of a metal storage facility. "The boat's at Whitman's Marina. Oh good, you know the place. You need her what? Oh, hang on." She took the phone from her mouth. "Mom, what's Jackie's Social Security number?"

Fran lit a cigarette and shook her head.

"It would be on your tax returns." Narrowing her eyes, she asked, "Wait, did you and Jackie even file taxes?"

Fran exhaled into the wind and squinted at the whitecaps building on the Bay.

"You would have needed her Social Security number to open a bank account or get a credit card. How do you pay for things, Mom?"

Fran glanced around the marina to see who might be listening. She didn't want others to know Jackie still had almost a thousand dollars aboard the Kittiwake. Fran's frugality made it possible for them to live on Jackie's Social Security check, which landed each month in Jackie's bank account in Vermont. Before heading south each fall, Jackie withdrew enough cash to make it through the winter. The big bills were in a Ziploc bag in the engine room, behind the fuel filter. A smaller amount for everyday purchases was in the cigar box glued to the dashboard at the helm.

Alice finished her call and started taking pictures of the Kittiwake and Whitman's Marina as if documenting a crime scene. "The funeral director said he'd notify the County Coroner when we find Jackie's Social Security number. He's sending two guys over here to take Jackie's body to the Tidewater morgue where the medical examiner will pronounce her dead. They'll come as soon as they ensure that they have the required personal protective equipment. Meantime, where's Jackie's will?"

Fran doubted Jackie had one. She climbed back onboard to see what she could find. After closing the door to the pilothouse, she popped open a porthole in the sleeping quarters to tell her daughter not to bother having the men from the funeral home come, but Alice wouldn't let her get a word in. If Jackie had written a will, she might have put it in the little safe next to the electrical panel. Fran didn't know the code, but she guessed Jackie would have used her sobriety date, 11-13. *Bingo.* The inside still smelled new. The manufacturer's warrantee clung from a strip of red tape. The safe was empty except for a gun.

"Nothing in the safe," Fran called to Alice, closing it back up and scrambling the code. "She didn't leave a will, but I know what she wanted. A simple burial at sea."

"These aren't pirate times, Mom. You can't just throw her overboard. We have to notify the authorities and follow protocols. Since she died intestate, her estate will have to go through probate."

As Alice identified the administrative tasks requiring copies of the death certificate, Fran filled her small watering can from the sink in the galley to revive Jackie's Christmas cactus, tenderly pinching off the dried flowers.

A boxy, black hearse approached like the shadow of a storm cloud in the parking area. Alice interrupted her list-making to greet it.

Fran reached into the back of the hanging closet for a large duffel bag. Then she accessed the compartment under the stern deck to retrieve her parka, winter gloves, and snow boots from a Rubbermaid bin.

Without asking permission to come aboard, Alice ushered the men in hazmat suits onto the Kittiwake. Fran began to object, but they pushed by, tracking clumps of mud from their boots. She shook her head and continued stuffing her winter clothing into her duffel while the men found their way back to the sleeping quarters. After a moment, the first one returned.

Addressing Alice on the dock, he asked through his respirator, "Where's the body?"

"Mom, what's he talking about?" Alice used her prosecutor's tone. "Where's the body?"

"Like I told you," Fran said. "Jackie wanted a water burial."

The VHF radio squawked with the Coast Guard performing morning drills. One of the men from the funeral home held out his gloved hand to help her off the boat. She handed him her duffel bag instead.

Reentering the pilothouse, Fran knew she had no legal right to Jackie's boat or bank account. She tugged at the curtains once more and stowed the last of the loose items before locking the door and lowering the Kittiwake's tattered pride flag to half-mast.

Alice consulted privately with the men for about twenty minutes in the parking area. When she returned to her SUV, Fran was sitting in the passenger seat with her shoes off and knees folded to her chest.

"You need to wear this mask and sit *all the way* in the back, Mom. There isn't enough hand sanitizer in the world…"

"Aye aye," Fran said to her new captain. She picked up Jackie's Christmas cactus and climbed over the console and the first row of seats with surprising agility for her age. Bending the wire in the surgical mask to the contours of her face, she added, "Turn up the heat, please."

Bronwyn Hughes is a certified public accountant currently working on her MFA in creative writing from Randolph College. She enjoys beekeeping, filmmaking, and boating on the many creeks and rivers feeding the Chesapeake Bay. Bronwyn lives in Tidewater, VA, with her partner and a Maine coon cat. Her work has appeared in *Atherton Review*, *Clackamas Literary Review*, *Evening Street Review*, and *Hawaii Pacific Review*.

CHARM BRACELET

Evelyn C. White

In memoriam, bell hooks
(September 25, 1952-December 15, 2021)

The first time we met, you told me that you operated
"on the outer limits of funkiness."
I committed your words to a scrap piece of paper,
carried it in my wallet
for years.

The next time, you (being you) told me that
my book was "deficient."
Thumbing through *Sisters of the Yam*
I delighted in your nod to *Sula*,
fast danced it into the revised edition.

The third (and final) time we met,
you side-eyed my new project,

insisted, "You should be writing about me."

Transgression was your charm bracelet,
your *hilarious* coin of the realm.

Evelyn C. White is the author of *Alice Walker: A Life*.

ELEGY FOR THE BEST DRAG QUEEN TO COME OUT OF THE APPALACHIAN MOUNTAINS

Sydney Bernthold

Take me to see the theatre in the park
Bring a bottle of wine
I want to sit in that elsyium grass with you
And park around the block from culture
When we can't afford to park in the lot

Tell me about Mexico
Describe those leviathan whales in dancing Spanish
Sip gin and tonic until
Como se dice en ingles
Your mother tongue slips away like sea foam
That hillbilly sound scrubbed out
Of your mouth
Like the thousand dollar sweater
Your mother threw in the dryer
Shrunk down to nothing at all.

Teach me about silk shirts and branded jeans
Teach me about how to park in the village
Teach me how to gossip, how to love your family in their complexity
Teach about the men you buy presents for and the one you married
(Always impressed by the way you knew the difference)

There was so much to learn
And I never took enough notes
I took for granted that I was never alone
Even when I was too
Queer, goth, strange, expensive, uppity

Too set on getting out of this little city
Surrounded by cornfields and small minds

All your friends came dressed as Anna Wintour to your funeral
My mother flew two thousand miles
Even the whales seem to miss you
The way they make their way south to live fully

    Sydney Bernthold (they/them) is an artist from Columbus, Ohio, and a recent graduate of The Ohio State University with a B.A. in English. They live in a haunted house with their gourami fish, Worf, and work various odd day jobs when they are not writing about things that go bump in the night. Sydney's work can be found online at *Neologism Poetry* and in print in *Star*Line Poetry*. They can be found online @sydneybernthold on Instagram and Twitter.

IRRESISTIBLE ANCHOVIES

Barbara McBane

Cedar Street

When we rented that apartment –
(was it a duplex?) we had no furniture.

It was big with endless shiny hardwood floors
tall windows in the living room and a fireplace.

But we had nothing at all to put in it
(living space was that cheap in those days).

When there were no furnishings for the flat on Potrero Hill
we painted pictures of curtains by the windows and rugs on the floors.

Cedar Street echoed so emptily we drove to a neighborhood
of mansions and found one with two huge cymbidia in
burial urns on each side of the porch.

The house was enormous (a private club?)
so even the urns looked dwarfish.

We parked and walked briskly up to the door
and stole the potted orchids one at a time.

It took two of us to carry each plant to the pickup.
(who would question two young dumb white broads in daylight?)

We put one urn on each side of the fireplace.

But it didn't offset the void so we laid out paper
and wood on the floor and built a kite as big as the side

of a container truck. We copied an image onto the kite
from a can of anchovies that said "Irresistible!"

with a woman lying on her back in a haystack
in a red-checked shirt open at the neck, sucking

on a long stalk of grass or hay or straw.
Then we took the kite to the hills
to see if it flew.

Barbara McBane is an independent scholar, media artist, educator, and poet living on Ohlone land in West Oakland, CA. She is an award-winning feature film sound editor and was Head of Critical Studies at the Pont Aven School of Contemporary Art in Brittany, France. She has taught film, sound studies, queer theory, and gender studies at the University of California, Santa Cruz; University of California, Davis; University of California, Los Angeles; and in Ireland. Her essays have been published in *Art Journal*, *Film Quarterly*, *Film History*, the Leslie Lohman Museum's *The Archive*, in film anthologies and art exhibition catalogues, and elsewhere. She holds a PhD from the History of Consciousness program at U.C. Santa Cruz.

VENUS

Josie Pierce

the only star we can recognize
from under the floodlights
in the backyard, burning grass,
my jaw cracks so hard it hurts

& what might have been already is --
in the dizzying swath of cloud,
dawn encroaching on the digital clock
so to say we are already lovers

though it is the first time,
we have in us what we could be,
hung umbilicals in the doorway.
I can't separate love from love from love

& want to cut everyone's hair.
what is the word for a person you love
who is not family or friend?
but something more infinitely attached --

kin or sister in the queer sense.
anyway not that we are like that,
but rather that my sister's sister's sister
could be your sister, who I recognize.

Josie Pierce is a poet/artist/butch-twink originally from Portland, Maine. She/he/they graduated from Sarah Lawrence College '20 and studied English literature at the University of Oxford. They have since served with non-profits in over ten different U.S. states. Their artistic concerns include revolutionary love ethics, anarchy, memory and nostalgia, God, ecology, and modernity. Pierce is currently a middle school educator in New York City, where they're working towards a Master of Art in Teaching at NYU.

YESTERDAY AFTERNOON

By Adela Zamudio (1854-1928), Bolivia
Translated from the Spanish by Lynette Yetter

To my sister Amalia

    After a hot day
came a cool fresh evening,
and in a delicious place,
sheltered beneath vaulted leafy boughs,
we paused.

    I lay my head in your lap:
you started to sing.
My gaze wandered by chance
until there in the twilight
we saw daylight expire.

    The sky was serene,
everywhere blue;
I leaned on your bosom
my heart full of peace,
listening to your song.

    The moon shone in the sky;
in its warm light I saw you
like an angel of comfort,
with folded wings,
who'd come to watch over me.

    Absorbed in your song,
I listened to you for a long time.
Your voice touched me so deeply,

tears poured.
I knew not why.

    So sweet was my sadness
that I pretended we were in Eden;
I raised my head then
and discovered with surprise
that you were weeping too.

    Maybe we both thought of
something at the same moment;
something we both remembered;
that's why together we wept
in the echo of your voice.

    The moon, clear and beautiful,
suddenly darkened.
Through vaporous clouds,
its dim mysterious light
poured enchantment.

    When I looked again
into your candid countenance,
like the moon,
it clouded for an instant,
and I saw your tears shine.

    Never in the midst of contentment
had I seen you so angelic;
that moment when
emotion illuminated you
with its heavenly flame!

Let's pray to heaven
that always united like this,
our song rises as one,
our weepings infused,
and that you never part from me.

Adela Zamudio (1854-1928) is Bolivia's most celebrated writer, feminist, educator, and social critic. Her birthday is a national holiday, and her collected works are one of the 200 most important books for understanding Bolivia. However, outside of Bolivia her work has been little known and mostly untranslated. Forthcoming is the bilingual book *Adela Zamudio: Selected Poetry and Prose*, translated by Lynette Yetter.

Lynette Yetter is a Pushcart-Prize-nominated poet who encountered Adela Zamudio's park and monument in La Paz, Bolivia, then wrote a thesis about her work for a Master of Arts in Liberal Studies degree at Reed College. Lynette Yetter's book, *Adela Zamudio: Selected Poetry and Prose*, is forthcoming. For more information about Yetter's music, movies, books, and art, you can visit www.LynetteYetter.com.

AWAKENING

Tova Vitiello

Daylight trembles in the room
where she squeezes
and shoves twenty-six years
into paper bags
and cardboard boxes.

She is tired
of cautiously arranging
his shirts, his socks,
her words.

She is tired
of long hours in the kitchen
the smell of gas
ready to explode.

This morning, she awakes
and reaches for the kettle
the one with scratches and dents
the one that doesn't whistle
as it sits on the burner.

For the first time,
she sees the walls crack open
and hears
the water boil over
while the heat of her womb
is snuffed out.

Tova Vitiello is a psychology professor emerita and a retired psychotherapist. She moved to Iowa City from the east coast in order to attend the University of Iowa where she received an M.A., M.S.W. and a Ph.D. Tova celebrated her sixtieth birthday by completing a six-month backpacking trip from Georgia to Maine on the Appalachian Trail. More recently, she explored the Galapagos Islands. As a political activist, Tova was a member of Women Against Racism (Iowa City), New Jewish Agenda, and the LGBTQ national Interweave (a Unitarian Universalist affiliation.) Tova is currently a volunteer at the LGBTQ Iowa Archives and Library. She continues to write and speak about social and political inequality. Tova enjoys being at her cabin and kayaking.

MICROTEAR

Jess Saldaña

The moment I forgot what time it was we were there together on the tracks that looked like a blanket of metal for the rocky ground reflecting a bright overcast I was delayed so I waited it was enough time for a crowd to form in the corner of my eye I felt something drip down and harden slightly the hardened part was painful to remove like when you first wake up and open your eyes there is a fine crust in the corners along with the waking the crust becomes remembered by the skin of your eyes and fingers who forget they have so much on them dirty fingers I try not to touch my eyes but I do anyway I forgot who told me that your eye skin is the most sensitive part of your face if you touch too hard it tends to tear these tiny tears microtears also used to describe what happens after a muscle gets physically worked I tried to look for the tears staring into the mirror at my face full of holes looking for any extra holes I might have made with my dirty finger the face is just a series of holes that absorbs everything in the wetness of conversation if conversation could tear my skin if I could absorb connection through my face could its sharp and soft places make contact with my eyes with other people's holes peep holes into other people's minds microtearing back and forth until the fantasy undoes both of us and you are you all over again crying at the train that is not moving a train that is not there there is a cloud that forms above you because it is that time of day you are weathering this on your eye skin just another hole where you can absorb things you were told not to things about tearing yourself up and about not touching who can and cannot tell you what you can and cannot touch do you remember it happened if you cannot remember who said it is it just the noise that comes with this time of days delay and these crowds that form in the corner of your eye who are all waiting for the same thing the same thing that is not there has it ever been there has it existed as you imagine it are you not even tearing a hole but just the idea of a hole that is contact with the outside skin of your dirty finger that worked a muscle scratched an itch you did not know was there forever if forever is as long as we believe it to be why must this train take forever to come if your face was not a face but just an archive of a series of holes a series of conversations if every word is a wound does every word itch when it heals do some words itch more than others do some words never heal going back and forth with your forgetful dirty finger on that place that feels so sensitive back and forth just like that what if the itching the scratching the picking is also somehow making love which is how you tend to make things how you tend to absorb really wet conversations that tend to tear you apart?

Jess Saldaña is an activist, artist, and scholar interested in interdependency within everyday systems and social relations. Trained as a musical composer, their poetry, fiction, book reviews, photographs, paintings, and drawings have been featured in the following; *Hoochi Media* (2018), *Stonewall's Legacy: Poetry Anthology* (2019), *Entropy Magazine* (2019), and *LAMBDA Lit* (2021), among others. They currently reside in Brooklyn amidst a clickety-clackety keyboard piano, piles of books, and their tuxedo cat Dr. Bear. You can view more and contact them at jesssaldana.com

NAME YOU

Mischa Kuczynski

What
is the word you're called
but the shape
made to carry you
from mouth
to mouth

Say mouth
and I see us
but the word was there
before we ever were

I have a want
to name you —

something someone
has never said —

a new mouth
a new sound
that feels what it is
to be the one you hold

but how can I shape
the sound
how can I hold it
without swallowing

FIRST KISS

Mischa Kuczynski

Awake,
every cell, a star,
opening and opening.

They didn't even know
they were sleeping.

Your mouth wakes them
and the world is at once
expansive
and impossibly,
perfectly small.

VESTIGIAL

Mischa Kuczynski

Is it that I
am one body
or two bodies,
one
without feeling?

It becomes clear
when our open
mouths touch.

I am one mouth
endlessly sucking.

Mischa Kuczynski is a queer Jewish poet and artist living in Northern California. She holds an MA in Creative Writing in Poetry from the University of California at Davis and a BFA in Studio Art from the University of Utah. Her work has appeared in *American Poetry Review, Gigantic, Fence,* and *Foursquare.*

THEM III

Sofia Ivy Ripley

   after Stacey Waite

: Dear gender /

    // I'm getting razor sharp
    on all your edges / I'm getting caught
    on all the branches that / stick up out of you

: Dear gender /

    // have you seen the way I glow when I'm asleep?
        I am everything /
    at the same time that I am nothing // no one
    looks at me /
& knows me

: Dear gender /

    // I want breasts /   I want
       other things I do not
   need /   I am a collection
          of selfish matters / of the flesh
          I hate
    all the ways you've failed me
    you / are a mean bastard
    I blame you / for not being
       what I want you to be

: Dear gender /

    //   I wake up in the morning
    & I am made of you /

>   you are only the good colors
> // maroon / night music / pink
>   of bubblegum or rose quartz
> that kind of / browning yellow
>   on a sunflower /
> // I am trying to teach myself /
> that a little is better than nothing

Sofía Ivy Ripley is a graduate of Florida International University and, as of a very recent move, a proud Chicago lesbian! She came out at the beginning of the pandemic and has been struggling to get back on her feet, but recently things have been looking up. She's fallen in love, she's moved to the big city, she might become a welder, and she's getting into kickboxing. Her work has been published in *So to Speak, Fjords Review*, and a couple of other places.

CAMP/PLAY

Shelby Griffin

I was born in pearls and moonlight, to ten mothers and one father and all of them loved me. Or perhaps that's just the legend. I was born on a stage, in a spotlight, with holy words on my tongue. I started speaking and champagne poured out of me and all my mothers had a glass and my single father sat back with a chuckle, "My girls." Of course, the possessive is inaccurate but even dreams have their structural integrity. I was raised to be a poet or a witch or a slut. I chose to look the other way. The wind blew me to the sea and my sister dragged me back home. All this to say, I have a flair for the dramatic. There is no such thing as true or false.

So here we begin our story, with an understanding of the impractical and improbable, and an application of glamour. Here's the real deal.

My mother and father were poor for generations. There was a son before me but he is long gone. There was a daughter after me and she is much taller than I. My father left and then he died. His ghost haunts our garage and we miss him terribly. This is not the story.

I was a fearful child and I learned silence was a virtue. I kept my visions to myself and suffered on the high holy days, like all other teenage martyrs. I found my way onto the stage and cried grief and grief and grief and grief. My directors called me chicken broth. This is not the story.

I fell in love with a brown boy-girl and we were married and then we fell apart. I hold my ribs together and call his name under the full moon. He does not respond. This is not the story.

Under a tree, I soak in the sunlight. The silhouette of a woman approaches me with a peach-scented aura and a do-good desire. I fall hard. The leaves on the tree rumble with understanding and lead me to reality. This is the story. How one whore may learn to trust another, writing each other's names with ancient tongues and cursed saliva. All of history turned backwards and rewritten in favor of the mystic supernatural. Here, we call it camp.

Camp is the beginning, indoctrination. Camp which is style over substance, an inherited curse passed down through filthy bloodlines. A way for the dregs of society to recognize one another and raise a church. Camp is a sanctuary to freaks and faggots. I met camp in the eleventh grade when she called me to the theater, holy arena, and asked me to dance. I felt her in red velvet curtains and red velvet lipstick. I met her through high school drama and high art. She held my hand and showed me the greats- *A Streetcar Named Desire, The Birdcage,* Bette Davis and Virginia Woolf. Camp is to glamour what logic is to understanding, more of a lateral move. However, after years of practice and graduation, I called myself Camp Supernova and moved forward without dignity, without grace.

This brings me to the middle. On the way to success, you lose yourself. I, alleged actor, turn on and turn out for all the wrong ideals. After the patriarchal death, there is an overwhelming desire for normalcy. This is anti-camp, this is submission. The system exposed for all its faults and virtuelessness. All that's left to do is laugh. Deep despair calls all of us to the brink of insanity. I cloak myself in traditional rites and bite my tongue, except for the lines to which I am assigned. I learn that honesty is for other people. I am concerned with performance.

"What performance?" you might say, so I'll tell you. A feminine dance of the seven veils which calls me out of myself and exposes all frayed nerve endings. There is the first layer, the dress, which is much too tight and clinging. Then, there is the skin, then the hands, with scales and talons and gloss. Next, there is the gut, bulging and bloated but starving still, surviving on a diet of grease and Milky Ways. The following tree trunk stilts, heeled, ruled by cellulite supreme, holding me up ironically. Eventually, this leads us to the core, slippery and evil, locked away for a knight to rescue and devour. And lastly, there is the wig, almighty symbol. Long raven locks which curl like snakes around a heart shaped face. In this way, I learn to be something I'm not, and I am damn good.

Anti-camp is a commitment to the falsity of institutions, playing along in a game you did not choose, as a means of avoiding the bloody pulp of yourself. When I first fell in love, I was not who I was. So what then? When you wake up locked in a body that is not yours?

Something saved me, a soft fleshy something. Something with curves, dripping wet. Ah, woman, you have found me. Dyke-camp belongs to the girls. It is all the places we are told to ignore. All the wet, gushy longing we avoid in favor of patriarchal approval. It is the glorifying of minutia, the excellence of detail. It is flowery misunderstanding and Avant Garde romanticism. It is the accusation of magic aimed at the bottom bitches.

When she holds me in her arms, the grave of my body is overturned and I rise out of me, like a criminal, into a second chance. We escape from what we know and we like it that way. We build a house for ourselves and we have no answers. But we are free. We are free.

Dyke camp is a call to the ultra-natural, return to the land. Mother earth is a dyke and she makes space for us all. The world's sapphic roundness pulls us close together, so we sing. The birdsong of unholy chosen women echoes through millenia and finally, finally we are not alone. There is no end in sight, there is no need. Only want in abundance.

When you turn into the light, you learn to forgive the ones who came before you. I forgive all my mothers for the tongues they cut out. I forgive my father, his ruling fist long rotted now. I forgive my sister, her feminine height. I forgive my first love, his tender imperfection, he could not have saved me. I forgive the ocean for its vast unanswers, the beauty is the point of it. I forgive the god I grew up with for his almighty lies, broken bread, spilled wine. I forgive glamour for her falsity and pretense, she kept me warm so long. Finally, ultimately, I figure out how to forgive myself, my ugly humanity. I make a believer out of me.

Ah, soft thing, be free. Love another woman. Hold on for dear life.

Shelby Griffin is an actress, poet, and playwright living in the Dallas-Fort Worth area. She has studied theatre at Tarrant County College and has appeared in several Non-Equity productions regionally. Her work as a playwright has been produced at TCC Southeast in the Festival of New Plays and workshopped at Arts Fifth Avenue. Her poetry has been seen in *Grief Peace* published by Bad Twin Press. She currently works for Hip Pocket Theatre in Fort Worth, TX.

FRIENDSHIP

Barbara Rosen

Couched in the garments of friendship
Our love hides its face
Yet longs to be free.
The veil, now and again, is lifted
Two piercing eyes, desire unhidden,
Seek and are sought.
Briefly a spark burns
Then the veil falls.

At night I dream dreams not allowed
In daylight I smile and call you friend
Passion is hidden yet joy is in my eyes
Have you seen it, my beloved?
Do you know and yet as I, pretend not to,
That we each seek futilely what together we have found?
We have avowed to each other
All but what we most desire
Let us cease this denial
And fulfill the promise of our eyes.

IT WAS DARK

Barbara Rosen

It was dark and my skin didn't recognize your sex.
Your fingers, alternatively firm and tender
Massaged my back, then later caressed it.
My senses became alive for the very first time
And joyously my heart sang out, it's you! It's you!
For it was dark, and my skin didn't recognize your sex.

It didn't know, so couldn't help responding
In the dark, to your fingers on my back.
Each day we'd laugh, forgetting the night before.
Thus dissociated friendship and sensuality grew,
Neither admitting the presence of the other,
Until friendship became love and sensuality desire.

Now in the dark my body longs for yours,
And in the light my eyes search for yours, futilely.
For one dawn, the dark and the light met
Making love seem impure and desire barren.
You gave one last caress
And left.

A PRECARIOUS LOVE

Barbara Rosen

You came to me with arms outstretched
Drew me to your ample breasts, and
As you smiled the sunlight stroked your hair.

We kissed hello, then kissed again,
And every kiss did ease my pain,
Do you know the joy you gave to me?

With laughing eyes you took my arm,
Your fingers playing in my palm,
My darling child, you are the world to me.

As you left on Sunday eve,
I pleaded with you not to leave,
"Without you I can't live till Monday morn."

You pulled away, your eyes grew dark
(You can so swiftly dim the spark)
You looked into my face with callous scorn.

"My love," you said, "my dearest love
Upon me don't depend
I'm like the tide which swells and dies
A song that starts, then ends."

OUR HEARTS ARE AS ONE

Barbara Rosen

I am drawn toward you
Though miles do separate us.
Distance, time, mean nothing
As I feel your presence and reach out
To pull you toward me.

I smell your hair, soon
To be entwined in my fingers.
I look deep into your eyes.
Time stops. Society. Convention.
They are as nothing, when
I am deep in your eyes.
Soft black velvet they caress me,
As you will/can not
Always aware of the limits
Of convention, of morality.

Our hearts are as one, why not our bodies?
All our desire, all our love, is contained
Within artificial bounds
Yet we know more love, more true morality
Than is found in many g-d given covenants.

Still, we are afraid
So we only play at love and at loving
And our frustrated desires give rise
To a million kindnesses
And a million hostilities.

ONE LESBIAN LIFE

Barbara Rosen

The preceding poems were written in the mid-sixties, when I was filled with the anguish of an unrequited love for a woman. Nothing in my life had prepared me for such a possibility.

Perhaps I should have known when I had crushes on my third and eighth grade female teachers; but so did many others. Or perhaps in high school when I decided to go to a women's college, but in those years, the late 1950s, homosexuality was not on my mind.

I did go to a women's college, Mount Holyoke, where during my sophomore year a rumor spread that two of our dorm mates were having an affair. The implication was, more or less, stay away from them. (Today, this same college openly welcomes lesbians, bisexual, and transwomen. The hard work of many over the years has made that possible.)

In my junior year, a friendship with a classmate grew, for me, into love and sexual desire. We had a sensual connection through lengthy back rubs. We talked late into the night and visited during college breaks. My feelings grew and, though I never talked about them, it became clear they were not reciprocated. The times did not allow confiding in anyone, so eventually my outlet became writing love poems. It took two more years before I, while reading *The Second Sex* by Simone de Beauvoir, finally said to myself, "You are a lesbian." But I was not yet ready to accept it.

I was a nice Jewish girl from a middle-class background who would marry a Jewish man, a doctor or dentist, and raise our Jewish children. I rejected being a lesbian and decided my feelings would not go beyond that one woman. For almost five years I futilely looked for a man to love, continuing to write poetry about my longing for a woman.

Because I was in denial, I did not know there were already activists in several states starting to fight for LGBT+ rights. The Mattachine Society, founded in 1950 in Los Angeles by Harry Hay, had the goal of fighting for the rights of gay men. In 1955, Del Martin and Phyllis Lyon founded the Daughters of Bilitis (DOB) in San Francisco. Initially begun as a safe social outlet, it became the first lesbian civil and political rights organization in the country. In the 70s, I had the pleasure of attending a DOB meeting at Del and Phyllis's home in San Francisco.

Even before accepting my lesbian identity, I had two encounters illustrating how the law fostered discrimination in the 60s. The first was when applying for a job after my first stint in graduate school. On the application form were the questions: "Are you an active homosexual?" and "Do you have homosexual feelings?" I was shocked this would be asked and knew I was lying when I answered no to the second question.

The second experience was more personal. In early 1969, after I had decided to come out, I told one of my best friends. She told me that although she had no personal problem with it, she might work for the federal government one day (she already had had a government job) and her association with me might be a problem. At the time, the federal government was still allowed to, and did, fire homosexuals. Losing this friend probably informed my decision to not reveal myself to future co-workers, or to teachers or fellow students during my many later graduate school years.

After college but before coming out, my focus rotated among working, dating men, and resolving my feelings for the woman I still loved. I travelled around Europe for several months and I worked for IBM for a couple of years. Finally, enough was enough so in early 1969, I decided I would enter the lesbian world. But I really did not know how. I didn't know any lesbians or gay men. I would occasionally go to Greenwich Village and if I saw a woman I thought might be a lesbian I would follow her for a while, hoping she was going to a lesbian bar. I know that sounds ridiculous.

Fortunately, I had heard about DOB. When I saw an announcement in The Village Voice for a DOB meeting, I jumped at the opportunity. That evening I met the woman with whom I spent the next five and a half years, going with her to my first lesbian bars, together witnessing the second night of the Stonewall Riots, marching in the Gay Pride parades, going to various meetings of the organizations that started after Stonewall, working again at IBM, and then living in California.

All the moving around during those years I now attribute to my trying to figure out how to live as a lesbian, my discomfort with being a lesbian, and wanting to be away from my family. Eventually we moved back to the East coast and I went to graduate school to become a certified school psychologist, work I did for many years. Still, I remained closeted during all these years at school and at work.

After five and a half years my partner and I parted and for the first time I lived alone. For the next four years, I dated many women, had one important relationship, and basically lived the life common then to most lesbians. Few older women were seen at the bars. Almost no long-term couples were seen, so I concluded that long-term relationships were impossible. Only later, when I met couples who had been together for decades, did I learn my conclusion had been wrong.

My life did not really start to settle down until 1978, when I met the woman I now call my wife. After 28 years of loving and living together we married in Canada in 2006, attended by many family members and friends. We had been lucky to be accepted by each others families, and remain close to the surviving members.

During these years, my wife had a very successful career as a lawyer, giving us many opportunities I never expected to have. I went back to school and obtained a Psy.D. in Clinical Psychology then opened a private practice in Manhattan. I joined the Board of SAGE and had the luck of meeting and befriending my co-Board member the late Edie Windsor. I joined several other Boards as well, as has my wife. Over the years we have been major supporters of many LGBQ+ organizations, wanting to help with the work still to be done to eliminate the remaining discrimination against us.

I have been very fortunate to have lived an active and interesting life. Revisiting these poems for *Sinister Wisdom*, reminds me of how unexpected turns in my life, including coming out as a lesbian, have shaped my life, although in many ways I have lived the life my parents wished for me, so perhaps it is not so unexpected after all.

Dr. Barbara Rosen, a retired psychologist, practiced both school and clinical psychology. After witnessing the Stonewall Riots shortly after coming out, she became involved in the LGBT and Feminist movements. She served on the Board of Directors of SAGE and the Feminist Press, and continues to actively support Democratic women candidates for national and state offices. Barbara was married in Toronto in 2006 to her long-time partner Patricia Martone. They have been together for 44 years.

SOMETIMES MY FRIENDS ARE ANNOYED BY HOW OFTEN I SAY "LESBIAN"

Fable Todd

sometimes my friends are annoyed by how often i say "lesbian"
"i'm a lesbian"
        "the moon is a lesbian"
            "my gender is lesbian"
    "i have this friend (who's a lesbian)..."
               "i'm a lesbian."
not only do i say it, but
i have a lesbian pride flag on my dorm room door
i wear a sweatshirt that says "dyke rage" at least once a week
my instagram bio is "i'm a dyke"
and my favorite selfie caption is "big dyke energy"

i say that i'm a lesbian a lot.
sometimes, it's because it's become a joke of how often i bring it up
sometimes, it's because it's nearly instinctual, to say it without even thinking about it
most of the time, however,
it's because "lesbian" feels like home.
it's because I was so lost for so long, and the first time i heard "dyke" used as a loving word,
i had suddenly figured out what i was supposed to be in this world.

i'm a very sentimental person, and i find comfort in a lot of things (baking cookies, pretty pens, the color pink, late night trips to target, bad jokes, etc.)
but the most comfort i've ever found was not in any friend group or in even the most ~sparkly~ of journals,
but in calling myself a lesbian.
a dyke.

because to call myself lesbian is to be home.
(as cheesy as that sounds)

Fable Todd is a young lesbian in their twenties attending college for psychology in upstate New York, where they work as a research assistant in clinical psychological research. They use they/them and he/him pronouns and came out as a lesbian at the age of twelve, and then came out as nonbinary at nineteen. When they aren't in class or working, you might find them playing card games with friends, doing art, or baking chocolate chip cookies with their famous secret recipe.

REMEMBRANCE: SUE PARKER "RAINBOW" WILLIAMS (1934-2022)

Rose Norman

Multidisciplinary artist, musician, and instrument maker Sue Parker "Rainbow" Williams died April 7, 2022, at the age of 88. Most of her feminist friends knew her as Rainbow, although in recent years she began to prefer Sue. She came of age well before the modern women's movement, and it took her awhile to find lesbian feminism. Art was her lifelong calling from an early age. She grew up in Shreveport, LA, an only child who entertained herself by drawing. Her mother, a single parent, worked outside the home, so she was raised by an aunt with two daughters who were like sisters to her. She described herself as having been "on a very conventional path, looking for the EXIT SIGN!"[1] She pursued her interest in art first at the Texas State College for Women, then transferred to the University of Arkansas, after reading about its new Fine Arts Center in a national magazine. There she met an architecture student, Chaz Williams. She said of Chaz, "Neither of us wanted to get married, but we wanted family (how gay is that?). We wanted to devote our lives to art, architecture, travel." She graduated in 1955, with a Fine Arts major with honors, and married Chaz, who had a year to go on his five-year architecture degree. After several years in the Air Force (Chaz's education was paid by ROTC), they wound up in Orlando, where they adopted first a daughter, Julie, later a son, Benson.

All along, she had been studying all kinds of art, getting a master's degree in crafts in Mexico (together with Chaz), where they learned clay, weaving, batik, woodworking, printmaking, silversmithing, bronze forging, and more. She credits that study in

---

[1] Interview November 9, 2013, at her home. Rainbow revised these notes for archiving.

Mexico with giving her the confidence to come out as a lesbian. Back in Orlando, in 1969 she started an alternative school called Stone Soup, working with a neighbor who was her first woman lover. The school lasted thirty years, and both of her children graduated from it. She also built a pottery shop in her carport and spent eight years making pots with messages stamped on them, then turned to woodworking, making dulcimers, a total of thirty-seven over the years. She taught herself to play the dulcimer and started a band, the Amazing Almost All Girl String Band, "two artists and two lesbians who could sing or play some outrageous feminist materials." They were the house band for Pine Castle Center for the Arts in Orlando, where she taught. They played traditional string band songs like "Shady Grove" and "Cluck Old Hen," as well as feminist songs like Malvina Reynolds' "We Don't Need the Men," and Rainbow's original songs, including "Amelia" and "I Am a Channel." Rainbow saved videos of the band performing at the Pagoda, and her handmade band banner hung in her house.

Banner hand made by a member of the Amazing Almost All Girl String Band.

Sue/Rainbow had found lesbian feminist activism at her first women's festival, the 1977 National Women's Music Festival, which had started in 1974. That is where she found *Lesbian Connection*, Holly Near, and consciousness raising. She and other Orlando NOW volunteers published *Changes* for eight years (1977-

85), first monthly, then quarterly. She learned how to put together a newsletter from the editors of Gainesville's *WomaNews*, and soon was swapping subscriptions with feminist newsletters around the state and the country. "Newsletters Were My Feminist Education" she titles a story she wrote much later for *Sinister Wisdom*.[2] She and a friend also started a Lavender Bookmobile in Orlando, a lending library mostly featuring books by Rita Mae Brown. NOW and CR groups met at her house in Orlando. She called it The Wimmin's House and also hosted monthly full moon gatherings in the backyard, as well as "witchy weekends" that included tarot readings.

Photo Credit: Rose Norman

A sign on the side of Rainbow's Florida Ave. house reads "Museum, Open Daily, 8:00 to 5:00."

In the 1983-84 winter holidays, she joined the Women's Peace Walk from Gainesville to Key West, a 540-mile journey that began December 17, 1983, and ended January 30, 1984.[3] She writes:

---

2 [2] Special Issue, "Making Connections," *Sinister Wisdom* 117 (Summer 2020): 125-26.

3 On the origin of the peace walk, see Kathleen "Corky" Culver, "Into the Grueling Duelings of Consensus Dances Sweet Meditation," *Sinister Wisdom* 93 (Summer 2014): 23-26. Culver writes about her experience of the peace walk itself in "I Get Dry With a Little Help From My Friends," *Sinister Wisdom* 123 (January 2022).

"Physically, spiritually, emotionally—it was the most powerful single thing I've ever done. It truly CHANGED MY LIFE! Part of our bonding was intense interaction day and night, CHANTING OUR WAY through blisters, breakups and makeups. This BAND OF POETS created every day a way of being."[4]

Photo Credit: Sarah Carawan

Posing, age 48, with the piece she exhibited at the 1982 opening of the Orlando Women in Art House.

Sue/Rainbow's lifelong passion for making art of all kinds was a major expression of her lesbian-feminist activism. In her Orlando

---

4 Revised interview notes, p. 7. The capitalization is a feature of her writing style.

garage studio in 1980, she produced a local art show coordinated with the national Great American Lesbian Art Show (GALAS), held in the Women's Building in Los Angeles. At the 1982 opening of the Orlando Women in Art House, one of her pieces was a three-mirror dresser with a female orchestra made of spool women playing instruments to a tape recording of Kay Gardner music. Many of her art works are collages or constructions made from found objects, such as cigar boxes, seashells, children's blocks, or broken musical instruments. Amelia Earhart is a favorite feminist icon, and her name or photograph appears often in Rainbow's work.

Rainbow in 2013 with some of the art displayed at her home/gallery.

Photo Credit: Rose Norman

In 1978, through *Changes*, she discovered the Pagoda, a lesbian intentional community and cultural center 100 miles north of Orlando in St. Augustine. She bought property at the

Pagoda and in 1984 moved there permanently. In St. Augustine, she enrolled in an architectural drafting class at a local vocational school[5] and for three years apprenticed with Dore Rotundo. Dore was a licensed architect and had sold her Pagoda cottage the year before Rainbow moved there. Dore's studio was in Melrose, and Rainbow worked with her there on designing a beach front house next to the Pagoda. At the Pagoda winter solstice celebration that first year, she took the name Rainbow.

Rainbow was very active in the arts while at the Pagoda, producing art shows as well as concerts, performing with her band, and going with other Pagodans to help Lin Daniels and Myriam Fougère with the East Coast Lesbian Festival (ECLF). For the first ECLF, Rainbow created a twenty-foot mural on brown wrapping paper depicting Pagoda women in characteristic poses, Myriam with her video camera, Nancy Breeze hanging sheets on a clothesline, herself playing a dulcimer. She illustrated (for free) both volumes of Terry Woodrow's *Lesbian Bedtime Stories* (1989, 1990). Rainbow's art was used on the cover of the brochure for the National Lesbian Conference in Atlanta (1991), as well as the ECLF brochure. While she lived in her North Pagoda cottage, she treated it as a studio and gallery, as she did her Florida Ave. home right up until her death. She made a YouTube video tour of her home and gallery and used it as her email signature, https://youtu.be/6my5UAHiFpk

---

5 Rainbow says she enrolled in the drafting class, then asked Dore to help her with some "isometric drawings." Dore offered her an unpaid job as an apprentice. Rainbow finished out her class but shifted her energies to the apprenticeship.

BOOK REVIEWS

Still Water: Poems
by **Jewelle Gomez**
BLF Press, 2022, 110 pages. $14.99

Reviewed by Sarah Heying

Most readers likely know Jewelle Gomez from her 1991 debut novel, *The Gilda Stories*, a genre-bending opus whose heroine escapes slavery, transforms into a vampire, and migrates throughout the US across two hundred years, forming a variety of queer networks along the way. Gomez was also recently featured within the pages of *Sinister Wisdom* 123 (Winter 2022) for her work with the iconic feminist journal *Conditions*, and her long legacy of feminist activism has shaped her diverse oeuvre: she has written plays, poems, essays, and fiction, all of which speak to Gomez's long-game vision of a more inhabitable, loving, and equitable world.

In *Still Waters*, Gomez revisits familiar questions of heritage, belonging, and radical love, infusing them with a complexity both burning and generous, wrought through the wisdom of hindsight and a lifetime of experience. The biographical material describes Gomez as a "playwright, novelist, poet, and cultural worker," as "African American," and as "Cabo Verdean/Wampaonoag/Ioway." These are only a few of the many words Gomez associated with her experience, and their relevance to her life shifts along with the ebb and flow of communal and individual need.

In "Coloured Lesbian Poem," Gomez processes some of the more old-fashioned ways of naming her experience that have been most meaningful to her, and she does so without disavowing her multiple ways of being. "Queer does help me remember / I am not alone in my slot," she writes, "But the slot is important too. / It's a nest carefully built over years / from twigs of history / and the blood from birth and wounds" (44). Twig-by-twig, letter-by-letter, and line-by-line, Gomez transfigures "coloured lesbian" into a home of her own, one that she built (with the help of very many others), shaping it around her winged body as a place to find comfort, to grow, to rest, and to be born again, and again, and again. Some nests remain, and some crumble over time. At a certain point, it is simply the pleasure we derive from a name that becomes its staying power. "I do love having choice," Gomez insists, before turning over the pleasures of "woman-identified," "woman loving woman," "same gender loving," and "queer." Still, her body tells her where her true love lies:

> But more, I love writing the words:
> A coloured lesbian
> is a coloured lesbian
> is a coloured lesbian […]
>
> And saying the words
> tastes good in my mouth
> just like that other word,
> you know…pussy!" (46).

When it comes down to it, some words are just more delicious than others, and what makes a word delicious is as complex as the person tasting it.

Some names we choose for the pleasure and connection they give us, and some we are given. As the final poem of the collection, "The Naming" renders the experience of being given a name by someone entrusted with the power. Jewelle walks into the poem, into the memory of gathering in a New England yard for a Wampanoag naming ceremony. This time she is granted a name not based on the desires of her biological parents, but on the energies that course through her at that particular stage in her journey. She walks out of the poem as "Still Water—for moving slow through stone, / leaving my trace embedded in rock, in sand, / on the pages of lives" (105). This name may not have been taken by choice, but it has been accepted as a sacred gift:

> Lifting my name from the air that
> whistled through the bare branches
> you lay it across my shoulders
> where it now sits
> as if it were always
> my own. (105)

The poet's name is plucked from the wind by someone who can listen—someone who sees the poet—and it settles gracefully onto the shoulders of their keeper. This kind of name is a loving companion, a reminder of the journey and its pauses.

"Still Water": a name suggesting the calm after a storm. There is an absence of movement, yet the memory of turbulent waters remains. Gomez notes that she met her namer, her "sister/friend," Mineweh, by her mother's bed, as her mother was "dying / with a grandeur lacking in life" (103), suggesting that one cycle's end was the beginning of another. In the preceding two poems, "More Than One" and "Pardo – Searching for a Name," Gomez confronts the lineage she discovered through her mother, her mother's mother, and her mother's grandmother. Gomez encountered a lot of pain throughout her relationship with her mother, a vivacious woman who left Gomez to be raised by her grandmother and great-grandmother. This pain often left her feeling like "the abandoned one / too dark for my mother," and, by extension, "too fat to work in television / too light for the Black movement / too kinky-haired for the tribe" (95, "More Than One"). Yet it was also her mother who sought out information about their Ioway and Wampanoag heritage and shared it with Gomez. Through this awareness of a deeper history, a deeper connection emerges.

Her mother, Dolores, was given a birth-name heavy with sorrow. At her own naming ceremony, she is eventually given a Wampanoag name meaning "Has No Horses" because "she had no need to go to people / they would come to her" ("Pardo," 100). On one hand, this sounds like a euphemism for "avoidant." Or in another more generous light, perhaps this name grants Gomez the chance to see her mother anew: as an unattached free spirit who attracts others to her. Gomez finds a new thread of contact with her mother, and, when her mother dies, this new thread helps weave a fuller memory:

> Say her name out loud
> and hear her laughter almost as warm
> as a story; big and round,
> full of pasts overlapping and
> contradicting each other.
> It's a name I'll remember
> now that the women,
> my small nation,
> are all gone. (100-101, "Pardo")

The sound of "Has No Horses" carves memory out of air, taking both the shape of laughter and loss. In turn, Gomez grants her mother another transfiguration by carving the shape of her name, sound, and memory onto the page, compelling the reader to "Say her name out loud." Go on—do it, and hear the big, round laughter.

Though her personal history is a central focus of this collection, Gomez hardly restricts her exploration of what it means to locate, remember, and name our histories to individual or familial concerns. In a poem dedicated to Lawrence Ferlinghetti, she calls upon poetry's power to render someone through sound and image, a form of memory-making that is both visceral and conceptual:

> What comes to me is
> the echo of a heart
> the thump of a drum;
> or your typewriter
> pounding out words,
> embroidery thread of life. (35, "Beats")

Echoes of memory that persist through sound; sound, which precedes the inked word and opens us up to the rhythms that carry us through life, death, and all. A poem renders sound, yes, and more: a poem is a stone, built from the sediment of words and line and rhythm. When Gomez casts Audre Lorde into a poem, she writes of Lorde as "a stone that has come to mean / both delight and death" (33, "Coal"), once again making room for the layers that a person's memory requires. Though a stone may seem solid and unchanging, it is only one form at one point in a long, ongoing story of change. Gomez's memory-poems do not simply preserve a legacy—they perform "a transubstantiation, / more important than that of myth" (34). To create and hold space for a memory's movement is to honor its continued, evolving existence among us, whether we are naming it or not.

For as much as this collection explores the processes by which we find words to describe ourselves, it is telling that the opening poem does not explicitly name a particular person, but instead a date: "January 20, 2021." This poem's vivid clarity paves an unassuming path toward transcendence, while simultaneously packing the gut-punch of reality's ongoing violence. In naming the day and not the inaugurated President, Gomez gives power to the collective feeling surrounding a pivotal moment, rather than further glorifying the individual man who stands in as an idol of the people's power. Like many symbols, the President's power can be both more and less potent than it initially seems. "We've painted many pavements yellow and / black, talismans to ward off evil," Gomez reflects. "Yet they draw evil to them, rollers in hand / As if making something invisible is possible" (11). Symbols, words, and poems can certainly make empty promises, and it can become easy to feel disillusioned with their worth. Still, it's also easy to recognize their power in the adamant, continued violence that tries to make us believe our erasure is possible.

> The true revolution will be you embracing
> your shame, bubbling beneath the crust of history.
> Rising in a plume of fire and tears and
> rocks crystalized with anguish.
>
> Lava must flow sudden and scalding,
> burning off false histories,
>
> Making you tough enough to recognize
> lies when you hear them. (12)

Our pith always remains, and it is a beautifully complicated, ever-evolving stone of many layers. Sometimes, it just takes a fire to remember.

god must be a boogie man
by **Nancy Klepsch**
recto y verso, 2018, 66 pages. $11.99

Reviewed by Ivy Marie

Nancy Klepsch's debut poetry collection, *god must be a boogie man*, is a stew of politics, technology, religion, history, and social commentary, the heaviness of which is diluted with nourishment and ritual.

Klepsch is the cook who commands the reader to "part your lips" so that she can ladle her poems inside. Or Klepsch is the jazz lover, knees trembling while B.B. King "start[s] a fire in [her] broken bones." Or Klepsch is the protestor critiquing gay stereotypes in "Queer Folk," reproductive injustice in "Non-repro Blues," and racial discrimination in "Green Book." Or Klepsch is the healer pleading the reader to "tell [her] you're beautiful," that the reader will "always eat organic rice," that the reader will always take care, even with death and pain and change and injustice happening all around.

Mostly, though, Klepsch is "stir-frying joy," wondering "how much pleasure a mouth can / Bring to someone as ordinary as dinner." She speaks in recipes and ingredients; to read this collection is to dine, every line a tasty morsel. Her prowess really shines in poems like "HEAD scout" and "Sweet Ones / My Potatoes," where she balances bitter reality with rich language; or "Truth or Fake Quiz" and "DIRTROAD," which play around with poetic presentation to gratifying results. Klepsch revels in storytelling, truth baring, and intimacy sharing, inviting readers to devour her work.

Like its musical namesake by Joni Mitchell, *god must be a boogie man* is complicated but true, brutal but tender, dark and full of raw, authentic life, and incredibly satisfying.

Sinister Wisdom
A Multicultural Lesbian Literary & Art Journal

SUBSCRIBE TODAY!

Subscribe using the enclosed subscription card or online at
www.SinisterWisdom.org/subscribe using PayPal

Or send check or money order to
Sinister Wisdom - 2333 McIntosh Road, Dover, FL 33527-5980

Sinister Wisdom accepts gifts of all sizes to support the journal.

Sinister Wisdom is free on request to women in prisons
and psychiatric institutions.

Back issues available!

Sinister Wisdom **Back Issues Available**

126 Out of Control ($14)

125 Glorious Defiance / Work by Disabled Lesbians ($14)

124 Deeply Held Beliefs ($14)

123 A Tribute to Conditions ($14)

122 Writing Communities ($14)

121 Eruptions of Inanna ($17.95)

114 A Generous Spirit ($18.95)

108 For The Hard Ones
   Para las duras ($18.95)

107 Black Lesbians—
   We Are the Revolution! ($14)

103 Celebrating the Michigan Womyn's Music Festival ($12)

102 The Complete Works of Pat Parker ($22.95)
   Special Limited edition hardcover ($35)

98 Landykes of the South ($12)

96 What Can I Ask ($18.95)

91 Living as a Lesbian ($17.95)

88 Crime Against Nature ($17.95)

80 Willing Up and Keeling Over

49 The Lesbian Body

48 Lesbian Resistance Including work by Dykes in Prison

47 Lesbians of Color: Tellin' It Like It 'Tis

46 Dyke Lives

43/44 15th Anniversary double-size (368 pgs) retrospective

- Sister Love: The Letters of Audre Lorde and Pat Parker ($14.95)

- Notes for a Revolution ($14)

Back issues are $6.00 unless noted plus $3.50 Shipping & Handling for 1st issue; $1.00 for each additional issue.
Order online at
www.sinisterwisdom.org

Or mail check or money order to:
Sinister Wisdom
2333 McIntosh Road
Dover, FL 33527-5980